COOK THIS

COOK THIS

Recipes for the goodtime girl

AMY ROSEN

RANDOM HOUSE CANADA

Random House Canada and colophon are trademarks.

www.randomhouse.ca

National Library of Canada Cataloguing in Publication

Rosen, Amy
    Cook this : recipes for the goodtime girl / Amy Rosen.

ISBN 0-679-31257-9

    1. Cookery. I. Title.

TX714.R662 2004   641.5   C2003-906778-5

Drawings by Paul Davis

Text design by Daniel Cullen
Cover design by CS Richardson

Printed and bound in Canada

10 9 8 7 6 5 4 3 2 1

Contents

ACKNOWLEDGEMENTS
Special Shout-Outs

A big thank you to my first editor, the great Sarah Davies, who got the ball rolling—and then moved to Haiti (of all things!). I'm also feeling loads of respect and affection for my current editor (and all-around fabulous girl), Tanya Trafford, who picked the ball back up, ran with it, almost finished the gig—and then got pregnant and had a baby (of all things!). And my undying gratitude to that brilliant Brit, Paul Davis, for his remarkable illustrations and for turning my crazy vision into my dream book—and for not running off to Haiti or getting pregnant. I also think Daniel Cullen did a bang-up job with the book design. Let's hear it for Daniel!

General Thanks

To the following family, friends, colleagues and mentors, who all helped in the production of this book by either eating my food, offering ideas and support or, more often than not, providing some good, honest heckling: Mom and Dad, David, Marty, Andrew, Bubi Fran, Sean, Judi, Deborah, Madeline, Emily, Isaac, Michael H., Natasha, Joanna, Janet, Shragit, Steve, Tamara, Dave, Miriam, Ilona, Erin, Kirk, Tammi, Marci, Rob, Beth M., Matt, Beth G., Josette, Devin, Lorraine, Rebecca, Chris, Charlene, Arjun, Evan, Irit, Avi, Josh, Alan, Marilyn, Jessica, Garry, Linda, Toby, Hannan and Hartley. And to chocolate: for being there when I needed you most.

I know what you're thinking: this book is crazy. Is it a gourmet cookbook or a comic strip? An entertaining guide or quick-eats tome? Actually, it's all of the above and then some. And since this is *my* book, it's also full of my personal favourites, which include fine French eats, streamlined Japanese vittles, as well as high-carb treats and low-cal faves. However, you will find no recipes containing pears, fennel, headcheese or any other oddly textured or licorice-flavoured foods, for I hate them. My book, my rules. Besides, I think you're going to like things my way.

Take a read-through, enjoy the witty illustrations, get the lowdown on the different themes and see what piques your interest. Dog-ear recipes you might want to try later. Tear out any pages that don't appeal to you and mail them to enemies. After you read the "I Burn Water" chapter and learn about what you need to buy and know to get going (not much!), call your mom—tell her you're thinking about taking up cooking. Don't get upset when she tells you to keep the phone numbers for fire, ambulance and poison control at the ready. She's your mother—she worries about you!

This book is fun, but that doesn't mean it's not also a serious cookbook. This is where you're going to learn how to roast a perfect chicken and side it with homemade cognac gravy. It is here that you shall master chocolate crème brûlée and corn fritters from scratch. Within these pages is everything you will need to know in order to mix the perfect cocktail and throw a dazzling party. Sweet potato gnocchi? Mu shu vegetables? Indian butter chicken? Soon you'll be able to say, Been there, done that. The origins of Cajun cooking? You'll know soon enough. How to do trailer-livin' right? That's in here too. Recipes to stave off hunger, satiate cravings, save time, amaze family and friends. In. This. Book.

So what are you waiting for, a personalized invitation? Crack the spine and come on in. The cooking is fine.

I BURN WATER:
A cheat sheet for the novice chef

There are certain things your mom and dad should have taught you but didn't, because they weren't around enough, or because you didn't care to learn, or because they just didn't love you. Whatever the reason, it's time to stop blaming others for your problems and get your life on track. Here's how to get cooking. The rest you'll have to deal with on your own dime.

MINIMAL INVESTMENT FOR THE TRANSIENT CHEF

I have the least amount of pots, pans and kitchen utensils of anyone I know, which doesn't make much sense, being a cookbook author and all, but there you go. The reasons? First of all, I'm cheap. More importantly, though, I'm thinking of you, dear reader, and in creating my recipes I try to envision what you might have lying around your tiny galley kitchen. Besides, I hate clutter and I let only the good stuff stick around. Warped pan? To the curb. Used the yogurt maker only once? Off you go to the Salvation Army. Cut-rate salad spinner almost take out an eye? Feh. You really only need to invest in a couple of fistfuls of cookery equipment to pull off just about every recipe in this book. And if you don't feel like buying a hand blender or electric mixer, borrow one. When you do go shopping, buy the best you can afford, and your equipment will pay you back in spades. Here's a complete list:

2   saucepans with covers: one large (3 quarts) and one small (1 1/2 quarts)
2   frying pans (a.k.a. skillets): one large (10–12 inches) and one small (7–8 inches)
1   cast-iron frying pan
1   big pasta or soup pot (8 quarts)
1   wok
1   kettle
1   set of measuring cups
1   measuring pitcher (at least 4 cups)
1   set of measuring spoons
1   set of mixing bowls
1   salad spinner
1   roasting pan
1   meat thermometer (and a deep-fat thermometer if you're feeling fancy)

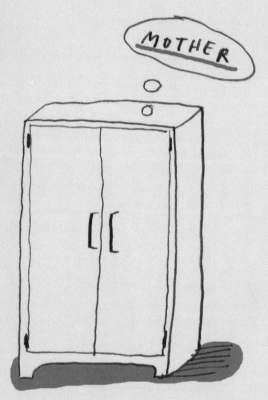

1	8- or 9-inch square baking pan
1	7- x 11-inch baking dish
1	9-inch springform pan
1	6-cup (not jumbo) muffin tin
1	wire cake rack
2	nonstick cookie sheets
1	spatula
1	wire whisk
1	soup ladle
1	pair of tongs
1	pastry brush
1	large stirring spoon
1	slotted spoon
1	long wooden spoon
1	large cutting board
1	small cutting board
1	colander
1	chef's knife
1	paring knife
1	small serrated knife
1	bread knife
1	grater
1	vegetable peeler
1	sieve
1	can opener
1	bottle opener
1	corkscrew
1	hand blender
1	electric mixer
2	ice cube trays
4	dish towels
1	pair of leopard-print oven mitts
1	French maid–style apron

WHAT MOTHER HUBBARD
SHOULD HAVE HAD IN HER CUPBOARD

Along with fresh groceries in the fridge (as in milk, eggs, fish, meats, cheese, fruits and veggies and herbs), this is what I would stock my kitchen cupboards with if I wasn't so lazy and disorganized:

FOR BAKING:
Chocolate chips, unsalted butter (buy it in sticks and keep it in the freezer), sugar, honey, cocoa powder, ground cinnamon, brown sugar, cornstarch, sweetened condensed milk, graham cracker crumbs, cornstarch, pure vanilla extract, all-purpose flour, baking powder, baking soda, cornmeal, biscuit mix, digestive biscuits.

OILS, VINEGARS AND CONDIMENTS:
Olive oil, vegetable oil, sesame oil, cooking spray, Tabasco sauce, margarine, red wine vinegar, white vinegar, balsamic vinegar, Dijon mustard, capers, gherkins, soy sauce, ketchup, mayonnaise.

DRIED GOODS, SPICES AND OTHER THINGS THAT KEEP:
Cumin, curry powder, coriander seeds, cayenne, sea salt, kosher salt, table salt, garlic powder, paprika, black peppercorns, mustard powder, chili flakes, bay leaves, dried rosemary, ground ginger, rice, cooking onions, shallots, garlic, canned tomatoes, tomato paste, crackers, real maple syrup, grated Parmesan cheese, canned chickpeas, breadcrumbs, potatoes, pareve soup mix, peanut butter, couscous, dried apricots, dried pasta, canned tuna, canned salmon, coffee, tea and me.

KITCHEN AND CLEANING SUPPLIES:
All-purpose cleaning spray, paper towel, foil, pot scrubber, dish detergent, sandwich bags, plastic wrap, parchment paper, hand soap, sponges, trash bags, small fire extinguisher, napkins, a cleaning woman.

A WOMAN WHO DOES

SOME SCARY CULINARY
TERMS THAT MIGHT COME IN HANDY

I've tried to keep everything on the low-down, but you may read some cooking terms that could have you hightailing it out of the kitchen. And we wouldn't want that. So calm down and dry those pee-pee eyes. Here's a mini culinary dictionary.

À la minute: Prepared just before serving.

Al dente: An Italian phrase meaning "to the tooth," which describes the bit of give your pasta should have when bitten into.

Bake: To cook by dry heat in a preheated oven.

Baste: To spoon liquid over food while it cooks, adding flavour and moisture.

Beat: To mix with brisk, regular motion, introducing air and making the mixture lighter.

Blanch: To immerse food in boiling water for a short time, then drain it and rinse with cold water.

Boil: To cook in steaming liquid in which the bubbles are breaking the surface (212°F).

Chop: To cut into coarse pieces.

Cream: To beat ingredients together, usually butter and sugar, until the mixture is smooth, cohesive and creamy. Takes a bit of elbow grease.

Cut in: To mix a solid, cold fat, like butter, with dry baking ingredients until they form a coarse, meal-like consistency.

Deglaze: After meat or fish has been pan-fried and excess fat removed, a small amount of liquid (usually wine or stock) is added to the pan to loosen yummy browned bits from bottom. This becomes the base for a sauce.

Dice: To cut into tiny cubes.

Dredge: To coat with flour or another dry coating and seasonings.

Emulsify: Think back to your grade 6 science-fair project. Generally refers to using an ingredient to bind together usually non-combinable ingredients, like oil and water. Egg yolks, which contain the natural emulsifier lecithin, are the most common emulsifying agent used by the home chef.

Fillet: A thin, long, boneless portion of meat or fish.

Fold in: To add one ingredient to the centre of a batter or mixture and cut down through the bottom with the edge of a spatula, gently lifting from the bottom to the top in a repeating motion until mixture is blended.

Garnish: To decorate the dish or plate for eye appeal.

Julienne: To slice foods into match-like strips.

Meringue: A stiffly beaten mixture of egg whites, sugar and flavouring.

Mince: To cut food into the finest dice possible.

Purée: To blend until smooth or to press food through a sieve to make smooth.

Reduce: Sounds like what it is—reducing a liquid by boiling it hard so that it reduces via evaporation, thereby intensifying the flavour.

Sauté: To cook food quickly in a small amount of fat over medium-high heat.

Sear: To brown surface quickly at a high heat. Usually refers to meat or seafood.

Simmer: To cook in liquid at a temperature that is just below boiling.

Skim: To remove the film that forms on the surface, as in some soups.

Steam: To cook over or surrounded by steam.

Stew: To cook in a small amount of simmering liquid for a long time.

Stock: Clear broth, a liquid by-product of cooking meat, fish or vegetables in a pot of water. You can also buy powder, bouillon cubes or concentrated gel and add to water.

Whip: To beat rapidly in order to increase the volume of a mixture by incorporating air.

WHAT THE WELL-DRESSED BAR WILL BE WEARING

If you're a minimalist, just buy the necessities. If you're a maximalist, build the bar of your dreams and stock it to the hilt.

THE EQUIPMENT:
Pitchers, a double-ended jigger, a variety of highball, lowball and cocktail glasses, a martini shaker, a long stirrer like a wooden spoon, measuring spoon set, measuring cup, corkscrew, bottle opener, can opener, ice bucket, ice tongs, small cutting board, paring knife, blender, toothpicks, coasters, sexist cocktail napkins, straws (long and short), tiny umbrellas, swords and swizzle sticks.

And you'll obviously need **BOOZE:**
Buy the basics (duty free if you can). The following list will enable you to make a broad range of tipples: a bottle each of Scotch, whisky, gin, dry vermouth, sherry, vodka, rum and brandy. Keep a goodly amount of wine and champagne on hand as well.

MIXERS: a bottle each of club soda, tonic water, Coke, 7-Up, ginger ale.

OTHER STUFF: grenadine, Tabasco sauce, Worcestershire sauce, angostura bitters, a jar of fat olives, sugar, fresh lemons, oranges and limes, maraschino cherries and loads of ice.

The BEST BAR NONE

SMOOTHING THINGS OVER AT WORK:
Turning office enemies into water-cooler buddies

You really did it this time: you screwed the boss, then he screwed you over, now everyone in the office hates you and you've got to try to win back their affection because work has become intolerable. Nothing says lovin' like a fresh pot of coffee and a mini fridge full of home cooking.

ROLLED VEGETABLE SUSHI:
Show Me the Maki

—

Serves 4

1 cup	short-grain rice
1/2 tsp	salt
1/3 cup	rice vinegar
1 tbsp	mirin*
6	sheets nori**
1/2	English cucumber, peeled and cut in long, thin slices (discarding seedy parts)
2	carrots, peeled and cut in long, thin slices
1	avocado, cut in half and sliced in thin wedges (prepare right before using so it doesn't turn brown)
3	green onions, sliced in half lengthwise
2 tbsp	sesame seeds, toasted
	Wasabi*** and soy sauce for dipping

SPECIAL TOOL
Sushi mats can be bought in Asian markets. You can use a 10-inch-square piece of BBQ-strength foil if you don't have a mat.

All sushi really amounts to is vinegared rice, vegetables and seaweed, with spicy wasabi and soy sauce for added zip and kick. Doesn't sound like much, but just like some other Japanese inventions, it's compact, it's high in quality and it will make you look like an artist.

1. Put rice in a large bowl and very slowly fill the bowl with cool water until the water is no longer cloudy. Soak rice in clear water for 30 minutes, then drain.
2. In a medium saucepan, bring 2 cups of water and the salt to a boil. Add drained rice, lower heat and simmer, covered, for 10 minutes. Remove from the heat and let sit, still covered, for another 10 minutes.
3. I'm thinking now would be a great time to prepare the vegetables. Slice away, nice and thin.
4. Return the rice to the bowl and pour on the vinegar and mirin. Mix it up well, using a gentle folding motion to cool down the rice. The more you mix, the faster it will cool.
5. Now comes the sticky part—assembling the sushi. Have a dry cloth and a bowl of water standing by. Place a sheet of nori on a sushi mat. For each roll, use just over 1/3 cup of rice. Dip your fingers in the water so the rice doesn't stick

to your hands. Press the rice evenly along the short end of the sheet of nori. Lay a slice of each vegetable over the rice (or a couple of slices, end to end, if that's what it takes to reach both sides) and sprinkle with sesame seeds. Carefully roll up and seal the edge by rubbing a wet finger along it. Roll tightly in plastic wrap. Repeat to make five more rolls. Refrigerate rolls for at least 30 minutes.

TO SERVE:

Slice off and discard—or eat—ragged ends and cut each roll into about six pieces. Dip top side in toasted sesame seeds and arrange sushi on a Japanese-inspired plate (or a wooden chopping board). Place a couple of small mounds of wasabi at each end, and pour some soy sauce into a few of your teeniest bowls (or just leave the bottle on the table). Done! And you said you couldn't make sushi . . .

MOSHI
MOSHI

*Mirin is a sweet rice wine used as a seasoning.
**Nori are pressed sheets of dried seaweed, used as the wrapper for our sushi.
***Wasabi is Japan's answer to horseradish. It comes as a paste or a powder that you make into a paste by adding water. Sometimes it can make you feel like blood could gush from your nose. Don't worry, it won't.

MARRAKECH ALMOND BUTTER:
Ali Baba and the Seven Almonds

—

Serves 6

1 cup	almonds
1/3 cup	olive oil
1 tsp	honey
Pinch	cayenne
Pinch	salt

I visited a Berber house while taking in the Atlas Mountains in Morocco. As the sun was setting and another call to prayer echoed through the village, we gathered around squat tables, tore off pieces of Moroccan bread (similar to thick pita) and dipped it in local argan oil, thyme-flavoured honey and almond butter. There's no food like the food you eat during trips to Exotica.

1. In a small frying pan, toast the almonds over medium heat, stirring occasionally, until they smell nutty and are slightly browned but not burned. Set aside to cool for about 10 minutes.
2. In a food processor or using a hand blender, pulse almonds until mealy, then drizzle in oil, honey and seasonings, blending until the butter has the consistency of natural peanut butter.

TO SERVE:

Scoop the almond butter into your earthiest little bowl, sided by triangles of thick multi-grain pita.

ASIAN CUKE SALAD:
It's Crunch Time in Chinatown

**Better than a knife up the nose. (Get it? *Chinatown*?)
And this crunch is infinitely more satisfying.**

1	English cucumber, peeled and sliced
1 tsp	salt
1	red pepper, diced
1	green onion, minced
2 tbsp	rice vinegar
1 tbsp	sesame oil
2 tsp	sugar
2 tsp	soy sauce
1/4 tsp	cayenne or chili flakes
2 tsp	toasted sesame seeds (optional)

1. Place cucumber slices in a bowl and toss with salt. Put in fridge for an hour.
2. When time's up, rinse and drain cucumber slices, pat dry and toss them in a serving bowl with red pepper, green onion, rice vinegar, sesame oil, sugar, soy sauce and cayenne. Sprinkle with sesame seeds.

TO SERVE:
I'm not saying it's a must, but why not do a little interpretive dance as you set it down on the communal coffee/lunchroom table?

PASSING THOUGHT
Mini bottles of liquor: depressing, or "fun"?

EASY HONEY GARLIC CHICKEN WITH EDAMAME RICE:
For Dumb Clucks

Serves 4

8	skinless chicken thighs
1 cup	brown sugar
4	garlic cloves, minced
3 tbsp	soy sauce
1 tbsp	minced fresh ginger
1 tsp	mustard powder
1 cup	liquid honey
1 cup	long-grain rice
1 cup	edamame,* steamed (follow directions on bag)
	Salt to taste

*Edamame are soy beans usually still in their pods. Look for them in the freezer section.

Forget about Chinese takeout. Instead, make this quick workaday meal ahead of time. Then, while your co-workers are queuing up at the food court, you can use your extra time to take a catnap (or download porn on their computers).

1. Preheat oven to 350°F.
2. Rinse thighs and pat dry. Place thighs in a baking dish large enough to fit them snugly. Evenly distribute sugar, garlic, soy sauce, ginger and mustard powder, then top it all off with a glossy coast of honey. Bake, uncovered, for 40 to 50 minutes or until juices run clear.
3. There are different schools of thought on how to make perfect rice. This is how I cook mine. You can do what you want. In a medium saucepan, bring 2 cups water to a rolling boil (this prevents rice grains from sticking together). Add rice, then reduce heat to a simmer. Cook, uncovered, for about 12 minutes or until water has been absorbed and rice is tender. Stir in edamame. Season with salt.

TO SERVE:

A couple of thighs per finger-licker and a big serving of edamame rice.

TIRAMISÙ:
Good for Me, Good for You

—

Serves 6

Never have soggy cookies tasted this good.

1. In a large bowl, beat together egg yolks and sugar until light and creamy, then beat in mascarpone until smooth. Set aside.
2. Dip half the ladyfingers in espresso and line a pretty glass dish with them. Sprinkle with half the liqueur.
3. In a medium bowl, whip egg whites until fluffy but not stiff. Fold into cheese mixture. Spread half the mixture over ladyfingers. Dip remaining ladyfingers in espresso, lay on top of cheese mixture and drizzle with remaining liqueur. Top with remaining cheese mixture and sprinkle with cocoa.
4. Refrigerate for at least a few hours, but preferably overnight.

TO SERVE:
Great mounds of gooey goodness. Dig in.

3	eggs, separated
3 tbsp	sugar
1	pkg (1/2 lb/250g) mascarpone or cream cheese
1	pkg (200 g) spongy ladyfinger cookies
1 cup	espresso or strong coffee, cooled
3 tbsp	coffee-flavoured liqueur such as Tia Maria or Kahlúa
1 tbsp	cocoa powder

GOODY BARS:
It's Hip to Be a Square

Makes enough for a party

1/2 cup	unsalted butter, melted
2 cups	fine graham cracker or Oreo crumbs
1 cup	milk chocolate chips
1/2 cup	Skor Bits
1 cup	chopped walnuts
1/2 cup	chopped macadamia nuts
1	can (300mL) sweetened condensed milk

This was the baked-good mainstay in my house when I was growing up. Be it for a birthday party, school bake sale, wedding shower or bris, inevitably my mom would show up toting some version of these sweet squares. Before I got the recipe from her, I honestly had no idea she was this lazy.

1. Preheat oven to 350°F.
2. Stir the melted butter together with crumbs and pat mixture evenly into a 13- by 9-inch baking pan. Evenly distribute chocolate chips, Skor Bits, walnuts and macadamia nuts over crust.
3. Drizzle entire can of condensed milk evenly over the top, then pop in the oven and bake for 25 to 30 minutes or until top is lightly browned.
4. Cool for 20 minutes, then cut into 1 1/2-inch squares. Let cool completely before removing squares from pan.

BAKING SIDEBAR
Make them your own. I added Skor Bits and macadamia nuts; you could add coconut and nix the nuts. Butterscotch chips or Reese's Pieces, pecans or white chocolate chips— think outside the square.

TO SERVE:
Get out the cookie tins and paper doilies!

SMOOSHED BANANA-CHOCOLATE MUFFINS:
A Half-dozen Snacks

Makes 6 large muffins

Better than cookies, kind of like cake, heartier than a doughnut (but not quite as sinful), muffins are the perfect snack for people on the go. This recipe is a one-bowl trick and makes half the muffins you'd usually make. Why? Because I only have one muffin tin. Who really needs 12 muffins anyway?

3/4 cup	all-purpose flour
1/3 cup	sugar
3/4 tsp	baking powder
Pinch	salt
1	very ripe banana, mashed
1	egg, beaten
1/4 cup	unsalted butter, melted
2 tbsp	milk
1/2 tsp	vanilla
1/2 cup	milk chocolate chips

1. Preheat oven to 350°F.
2. In a large bowl, mix together flour, sugar, baking powder and salt. Add mashed banana, egg, melted butter, milk and vanilla. Stir to blend. Toss in chocolate chips and give another quick stir.
3. Spray a 6-cup muffin tin with nonstick cooking spray. Divide the batter among the muffin cups and give the tin a bang on the counter to release any air bubbles. Pop in the oven for 25 to 30 minutes or until tops are golden and a toothpick comes out clean.

TO SERVE:
MMMuffins! Maybe the 1980s were good for something after all.

FOUR WAYS
TO MAKE THE
MOST OF YOUR WORKDAY:
1. Liquid lunch at the local Denny's
2. Vodka in Evian bottle
3. "Specialty coffee"
4. Beer fridge

SOLO SOIREE:
Quick bites to eat over the sink

Being home alone shouldn't always mean eating freezer-burnt Lean Pockets or microwaved popcorn for dinner. Take some pride in yourself, girlfriend. Because if you can't treat yourself to a home-cooked meal once in a while, what's the point of all of those appliances cluttering up the kitchen? Eat alone and love it.

CEVICHE:
Raw, Raw, Raw! Go Team!

—

Serves 1

3 oz	fresh firm skinless whitefish fillets (halibut, cod, etc.)
1	lime
1/2	avocado
1	small plum tomato, seeded and chopped
1	green onion, chopped
1/2	jalapeño pepper, seeded and minced
2 tsp	minced fresh coriander leaves
	Sea salt and cracked pepper to taste
	Drizzle of olive oil

You love this citrus-cooked fish when you eat out, so why not love it when you're alone? It's fast, more than delicious, perfect for your Atkins diet and the closest thing to an instant gourmet meal you'll find.

1. Cut the fish into 1/4-inch slices. Put in bowl and squirt lime juice all over. Stir to coat and let sit at room temperature for 20 minutes, until opaque.
2. When time's up, chop the avocado. Drain off liquid from fish and stir in avocado, tomato, green onion, jalapeño and coriander. Season with salt and pepper. Drizzle with oil.

TO SERVE:
Fork in fish, fish in mouth. Repeat.

CRABBY EGG DROP SOUP:
Sink Your Claws into This

Serves 4

With an upmarket kick from inexpensive canned crab, you've gone and made a favourite Chinese comfort soup that much more special. Look, I know I don't say it enough, but I'm proud of you. (And now you'll have three more meals of "soup for one"!)

1. Bring chicken stock to a simmer in a saucepan. Stir cornstarch with a little water to form a paste, then stir into simmering stock. Bring to a boil, then reduce heat to a simmer. Stir until soup thickens a bit.
2. Stir in crabmeat, peas and sugar. Simmer for a couple of minutes, then pour in beaten egg and give one more gentle stir. A little cracked pepper and you've got soup.

TO SERVE:
Ladle into one massive bowl and sprinkle with green onion. (Save the rest for tomorrow.)

4 cups	good chicken stock
1 tbsp	cornstarch
1	can (7 1/2 oz) crabmeat, picked through for cartilage and shell
1/4 cup	frozen peas, thawed
Pinch	sugar
1	egg, well beaten
	Cracked pepper
2 tbsp	chopped green onion

I'M CANCERIAN

LINGUINE WITH GOAT CHEESE:
The Best Damn Pasta in the World

—

Serves 1

3 oz	linguine or fettuccine
2 tbsp	olive oil
1	garlic clove, minced
1/2 tsp	chili flakes
3	oven-dried tomatoes (recipe p. 198) or marinated sun-dried tomatoes, sliced
1	marinated artichoke heart, chopped
1 tbsp	chopped fresh parsley
1	slice (2 oz) goat's cheese
	Sea salt and pepper to taste
1 tbsp	toasted pine nuts (optional)

Just because you're home alone doesn't mean you don't deserve to eat the best damn pasta in the world. I love this pasta dish because it's filling and the taste is divine. And that's why I declare it to be the best damn pasta in the world. Try it and see if you agree with me. You will. I know you will.

1. Cook linguine according to package instructions and drain well. While the pasta's in the colander, put the pot over low heat. Add olive oil, garlic and chili flakes; cook for a minute, stirring. Toss in tomatoes and artichoke heart; cook a minute more. Return pasta to the pot and toss together. Sprinkle in parsley and give another stir. Remove from heat.

TO SERVE:
Turn the pasta out into a bowl or onto a dinner plate and lay the round of goat cheese on top. Season with salt and pepper and sprinkle on pine nuts, if using. You can toss the cheese in so that it melts and forms a sauce, or nick off a bit each time you go in for a forkful of pasta. It's akin to the fruit-on-the-bottom versus stirred yogurt conundrum. To each her own.

STUFFING-STUFFED ACORN SQUASH:
Eighty-six the Turkey!

Makes 2 halves

All the great taste of a Thanksgiving dinner without the hassle of roasting a bird. It's a savoury meal in a squash shell.

1	small acorn squash
	Drizzle of olive oil
1 tsp	unsalted butter
1	shallot, chopped
1/2	McIntosh apple, chopped
2 tbsp	chopped celery
2 tbsp	chopped pecans
1/2 tsp	crumbled dried sage
2 tbsp	breadcrumbs
	Salt and pepper to taste
2 or 3	slices havarti cheese, chopped

1. Preheat oven to 375°F. Line a cookie sheet with foil.
2. Cut squash in half lengthwise and scoop out seeds. Drizzle the inside of each half with olive oil, then put cut side down on the cookie sheet. Roast for 40 to 50 minutes or until soft.
3. Meanwhile, in a small frying pan, melt butter over medium heat. Sauté shallot, apple, celery, pecans and sage until apple and celery are soft.
4. Remove cooked squash from oven, scoop out a bit of the cooked innards, and stir into vegetable mixture. Stir in breadcrumbs, salt and pepper. Re-stuff squash halves and top with cheese. Put back in oven until cheese melts.

TO SERVE:
Grab a fork and eat one half now. Go in for the second in about an hour.

SALADE FRISÉE AVEC PANCETTA ET OEUF:
To the French, This Constitutes a Healthy Salad

—

Serves 1

1	small head frisée or other curly lettuce
1	egg, poached (see sidebar)
1 tbsp plus 1 tsp	olive oil
2	slices pancetta
1	slice bread, crusts removed, cut in tiny cubes
	Salt and pepper to taste
1	garlic clove, minced
1 tbsp	balsamic vinegar

Why is it that the French can eat *pain au chocolat* and *café crème* for breakfast and *steak frites* for lunch, drink as much wine as they want, and still they have no thighs?

1. Wash frisée and pull leaves off. Dry well. Use about 2 cups' worth.

2. In a small frying pan, heat 1 tsp of the oil on medium-high. Add pancetta and cook until crisp. Remove pancetta and drain on paper towel. Add bread cubes to hot oil and toast, turning occasionally. Drain on paper towel. Season with salt and pepper.

3. Add remaining 1 tbsp oil and the garlic to the pan; heat for a minute, stirring. Remove from heat and swirl in balsamic vinegar. It might spatter, so stand back.

HOW TO POACH AN EGG IN THE PARISIAN MANNER

Bring a small pot of water to a boil, then lower heat to a simmer. Add a splash of white vinegar to the water and give it a swirl with a spoon. Crack egg into the vortex and after 5 seconds use a spoon to wrap the whites around the yolk. Cook for another 2 to 3 minutes (depending on how runny you like them). Drain on paper towel. Serve warm.

TO SERVE:

Put salad leaves on a plate, put warm poached egg in the middle and pancetta and croutons on top. Drizzle with warm dressing. *Mange tout de suite.*

OEUF la-la   'ALLO

ANGEL HAIR PASTA IN LEMON BUTTER SAUCE:
Instant Validation

Serves 1

This is a 10-minute cooking miracle, a one-pot wonder that leaves you with a sumptuous meal with no muss. Lemony, light and creamy without the use of cream, it's the kind of supper to make for yourself when you're having one of *those* days.

2 tbsp	unsalted butter
2 oz	angel hair pasta or spaghettini
1 cup	hot chicken stock
2 tbsp	fresh lemon juice
1/2 tsp	lemon zest
1 tbsp	snipped chives
	Salt and cracked pepper to taste
	Grated Parmesan cheese (optional)

1. Melt butter in a medium saucepan until it's frothy, then crack pasta into roughly 2-inch pieces and toss into butter, stirring to thoroughly coat. Add the hot chicken stock and give 'er a stir. Reduce heat to low, cover the pot, and cook for 10 minutes or until almost all the stock is absorbed and the pasta is cooked and looking saucy.
2. Stir in lemon juice, zest and chives, sprinkle in salt and crack in pepper. Stir it up and top with grated Parmesan if you like.

TO SERVE:

Plant yourself in front of the TV, pop in your *Breakfast Club* DVD and eat the pasta right out of the pot. Feeling better?

DINING TIP
This dish is particularly good as a midnight snack (or hangover cure).

CARAMELIZED POTATO, ONION AND BLUE CHEESE FRITTATA:
One Big-ass Omelette

Serves 2

1 tbsp	olive oil
2	medium Yukon Gold potatoes, peeled, halved and very thinly sliced
2	medium onions, thinly sliced
1/2 tsp	crushed dried rosemary
1/2 tsp	salt
	Cracked pepper
Pinch	sugar
4	eggs
4	egg whites (you could freeze the extra yolks and use them in the tart recipe on p. 176 the next time you feel your inner baker coming forth)
1 tsp	unsalted butter
3 oz	blue cheese, crumbled

Eggs are always there. They're the culinary friends you can always call on in a pinch, or just for a laugh. Eggs listen. When nobody else is around and the whole world has let you down, they're still there, waiting for you to get crackin'.

1. Pour olive oil into a large (about 10-inch) nonstick frying pan on medium heat, then lay in potato slices and onion slices. Sprinkle with rosemary, salt, pepper and sugar. Cook, stirring often, until well browned, about 15 minutes. Place vegetables in a bowl to cool.

2. Whip together eggs and egg whites. In the same pan, melt butter over medium-low heat. Pour eggs into pan. Cook eggs, pulling the edges in with a spatula, and letting uncooked egg seep to the sides. This helps cook the eggs faster and more evenly. After a couple of minutes, lay caramelized potato and onion over your omelette, smoosh them in a bit, and then sprinkle with blue cheese. Crack a little more pepper on there for good measure. Smack a lid on top and let the frittata cook for a few more minutes until it's cooked through and the edges are slightly browned.

TO SERVE:

Loosen with a knife and slide the frittata out of the pan, cut into wedges and dig in. You want ketchup with your eggs? We don't cast stones. But do me a favour and try it without first. You might be surprised. And a simple green salad with this makes it a *fait accompli*.

COOKING TIP

The variations for frittatas are as endless as your imagination. Unless you have no imagination. In which case, you're screwed. But for a jealousy-inducing lunch the next day, lay a wedge of frittata in a sliced crusty roll, spread with a touch of mayo, slices of cheese, lettuce and tomato, and watch the I.T. guy drool.

YOGURT WITH HONEY AND TOASTED PINE NUTS:
For Guilt-Free Desserting

Serves 1

1 cup	Greek or Balkan-style plain yogurt (at least 2% butterfat, please)
1 tbsp	good honey (the hoity lavender stuff you got in that gift basket would be perfect)
2 tsp	toasted, pine nuts

A great meal-topper for those times when you need something a little sweet but you don't have any chocolate in the house. (How did that happen, anyway?)

1. Get out a bowl, spoon the yogurt in, drizzle the honey over, sprinkle the pine nuts on.

TO SERVE:
I've got nothing more to say about this. Just enjoy.

SPICY MEXICAN HOT CHOCOLATE:
It's Soothing, It's Sweet, but It Talks Back

Serves 1

I never grew out of hot chocolate: I still have a mugful almost every morning during wintertime. Some may chalk it up to immaturity or chocoholism, but I consider it nostalgia for the iconic glass carafe on the avocado-green stove—brewing a cocoa-y reward for shovelling the driveways of my youth. This version has a piquant kick that's rated adults-only.

2 tbsp	cocoa powder
1 tbsp	sugar
1/4 tsp	cinnamon
1/8 tsp	cayenne
Pinch	crushed coriander seeds
1 cup	hot milk
	Marshmallows, whipped cream or cinnamon stick (optional)

1. Get out your favourite hot-beverage mug (extra points for cheesy logos). Scoop in cocoa powder, sugar, cinnamon, cayenne and coriander. Stir together. Pour in hot milk and mix well.

TO SERVE:

A little whipped cream on top sprinkled with cinnamon would be nice. A couple of jumbo marshmallows, even nicer. Dropping in a rustic cinnamon stick makes you my new idol.

DRINKS TIP
Don't drink alone. Bring an imaginary friend with you.

RX FOR PMS:
TLC for food cravings and mood swings

PMS is tricky. It means a different emotion for every woman, for every minute, plus a cornucopia of cravings. I've tried to include them all here: sweet with salty, fried things, crunchy nuggets, soothing bites. If I missed any of your favourites, sue me. Bitch! Sorry. All of these recipes are best served with a soupçon of ibuprofen (and a red wine chaser).

APPLICABLE SHORT STORY:
A Bloody Good Show

My best friend, Natasha, had called me, extremely excited about being cast as Helen Keller in her high-school production of *The Miracle Worker*.

After weeks of props construction, costume fittings and jittery rehearsals, the stage was set for Natasha's performance. It was the last big event before graduation, before everyone went off to various universities and new lives. She really wanted to leave a lasting impression.

The buzz of anticipation filled the auditorium as everyone filed in for the opening night of the Hebrew high-school production (in conjunction with Beth Tikvah Synagogue and Hebrew National Hot Dogs) of *The Miracle Worker*. My friends Janet and Joanne and I had scored primo seats—front row centre, so that Tash could hear us cheering her on. The lights dimmed, the curtain rose, and there stood Natasha the deaf-mute, looking out and above our heads, brilliantly in character. She loomed larger than life, even though she was dressed in a simple blue gingham dress wrapped in a white cotton smock. Much of her portrayal entailed smacking the help, screaming and jumping up and down. She was simply marvellous, making for a rapt audience.

Positioned as I was, I was likely the first to notice the red pinprick dot that suddenly materialized on Natasha's bottom. I whispered to Janet, asking if she noticed anything, but she said I was crazy. What Janet didn't know was that moments before Tash went backstage, she had confided to me that she had just gotten her period and had applied three super-maxis to her underpants so as not to confront any problems during the show. I had warned her that sanitary napkins worked best when used one at a time, but she wouldn't listen. She never did.

That pinprick quickly turned into two, at which point Janet grabbed my thigh and we went into hysterical fits of nervous laughter—shoulders spastically rocking, gasping for breath and crying our eyes out. Every so often, when I could bear it, I would look up to watch Natasha's excellent portrayal of the girl who said "water." But mostly all I could do was watch her bum.

She pulled at her hair, rolled around on the ground, leapt up on the table, and the two red dots were suddenly joined. She threw a chair, broke a vase, did a cartwheel, and the patch had grown into a silver dollar. She rallied on, overturning the table and ripping up books, the red splotch now the size of the local Yellow Pages.

By the time intermission rolled around, Natasha had rolled around enough that the back of her dress appeared half white, half red, glistening in the lights with crimson-coloured blood. A horrendous thing to happen to anyone, especially a teenaged girl, in front of three hundred friends and strangers. But it happened, and Tash didn't realize it until she exited stage left and the rabbi's wife informed her that she had gotten her period. Several dozen more well-wishers came backstage to offer the stricken actress their condolences—and tampons.

After a bit of a crying session, and a change of clothes, Tash, big trooper that she is, got back on stage to finish what she had started. Somehow buoyed by her humiliation, she was even better in act 2.

YOU HAVE TO BE SANGUINE ABOUT THESE THINGS

CHICKEN SOUP WITH PARSLEY MATZO BALLS:
Bubi Fran's Penicillin

—

Serves 10–12

1	roasting chicken, giblet bag removed, excess fat trimmed, chicken rinsed
2	parsnips, peeled, ends chopped off
2	stalks celery with leaves
2	large onions, cut in half
6	carrots, peeled, ends chopped off
1 tbsp	sea salt
	Pepper to taste
1	small bunch parsley (chop and reserve 1 tbsp)
1/4 cup	fresh dill sprigs
2	packets matzo ball mix (plus eggs and oil called for in instructions)

A bowl of matzo ball soup is like Jewish echinacea. In fact, do a double-blind taste test and I think you'll find this golden broth goes a long way in healing what ails you. Heart and soul.

1. Put chicken in a very large soup pot and pour in enough cold water to cover Clucky. With the pot uncovered, bring to a boil, skimming off the foam that accumulates with a slotted spoon. Reduce heat to simmer and add parsnips, celery, onions, carrots, salt and pepper. Simmer, partially covered and without stirring, for at least 2 hours (3 hours is better for richer flavour, though). Skim occasionally as foam appears. With about 10 minutes to go, toss in parsley sprigs and dill.

2. For a pristine broth, remove chicken, veggies and herbs from pot and set aside. Strain the soup through a fine sieve, or a colander lined with cheesecloth (or a double layer of paper towel). Return the clear broth to a clean pot. Discard herbs. Shred or slice the chicken, cut up the vegetables, and return them to the soup before serving, or serve a clear soup bejewelled with a couple of matzo balls and use the stewed chicken for chicken salad sandwiches tomorrow.

3. You could make matzo balls from scratch, but the recipe would be the same as what's in the

box; matzo meal, salt, and the addition of eggs and oil. So why bother? Just scratch open the box instead and add extra cracked pepper and the reserved chopped parsley to the mix to make them your own. Follow the cooking instructions on the box.

TO SERVE:

A ladle or two of broth, a few slices of carrot and parsnip, a bisel of chicken, a matzo ball and a sprig of dill if you like. Shabbat shalom.

DO YOU LIKE YOUR BALLS HARD OR SOFT?
Some people like the big fluffy variety while others swear that balls possessing a firm core are the only balls worth chewing. I like mine semi-fluffy and just large enough that they can be eaten in three bites. Yup, that, to me, is the perfect matzo ball. What the heck did you think I was talking about, anyway?

SALAD WITH ROOT CHIPS AND VINAIGRETTE:
Field of Greens

___

Serves 4

1/3 cup	extra virgin olive oil
	Juice of 1/2 lemon
	(about 1 tbsp)
1	garlic clove, minced
1 tbsp	minced fresh parsley
1 tsp	Dijon mustard
Pinch	sugar
	Salt and pepper to taste
1	bag prewashed mixed field greens that serves four
1/2	bag gourmet fried root chips, slightly crushed (about 2 cups)

This is the perfect combo of mowing down on chips in front of the TV *and* eating your leafy greens.

1. In a small bowl, whisk together olive oil, lemon juice, garlic, parsley, mustard, sugar, salt and pepper. Taste, make sure you love it, then set aside.
2. Get out a big salad bowl. Open the bag of greens and pour them into the bowl. Open the bag of root chips and set aside.

TO SERVE:

It's important to toss this right before serving, for nobody likes a soggy salad. The good thing about the root chips is that they're heartier and sturdier (and tastier) than regular potato chips. So, give the vinaigrette another whisk, drizzle it over the salad, toss, pour on the root chips, toss again and dish it out.

CRISP SALMON CAKES ON ARUGULA:
A Light Lunch for Gals on the Go

Serves 4

This dish uses up the canned salmon you never thought would see the light of day, and those jars of capers and gherkins wasting away on the bottom shelf of the fridge door. Along with the Worcestershire sauce you've used once and the breadcrumbs (you're not sure how they came to rest in your cupboard), you've got a little luncheon that's as healthy as it is tasty. Plus, you've emancipated your pantry.

1. In a bowl mix together salmon, 1/2 cup of the breadcrumbs, egg, mayo, capers, gherkins, onion, Worcestershire, lemon zest, Tabasco and a few grinds of pepper. Form into eight nice little patties. Coat with remaining 1/4 cup of breadcrumbs. Set aside.

2. Wash and dry arugula and tear into bite-sized pieces. Toss with olive oil and a pinch of sea salt and some pepper. Set aside.

3. In a large frying pan on medium-high heat, heat vegetable oil. Fry a few salmon cakes at a time until golden on each side, turning once. This will take a few minutes.

TO SERVE:

Divide arugula salad among four plates and top with a couple of crispy salmon cakes and a wedge of lemon for squirting. A loaf of crusty bread on the side is almost a must.

2	cans (7 1/2 oz) sockeye or pink salmon, drained, skin and bones picked out
1/2 cup plus 1/4 cup	dry breadcrumbs
1	egg, beaten
2 tbsp	mayonnaise
1 tbsp	chopped drained capers
1 tbsp	minced gherkins
1 tbsp	minced red onion
2 tsp	Worcestershire sauce
1 tsp	lemon zest
Dash	Tabasco sauce
	Cracked black pepper
1	big bunch arugula
1tbsp	olive oil
	Sea salt and pepper to taste
2 tbsp	vegetable oil
1	lemon, cut in wedges, for garnish

OVER-THE-TOP CAESAR:
A Gutsy Version of a Favourite Salad

—

Serves 4

Croutons:

2 tbsp	olive oil
1	garlic clove, crushed
5	slices baguette, cut in 1/2-inch cubes

Dressing:

2	garlic cloves, minced
1	egg yolk
1 tbsp	fresh lemon juice
1/2 tsp	lemon zest
1 tsp	Worcestershire sauce
1/4 tsp	sugar
1/4 tsp	mustard powder
1/4 tsp	salt
1/4 tsp	cracked pepper
1/3 cup	extra virgin olive oil

Fricos:

1/2 cup	freshly grated Parmesan cheese (must be freshly grated or won't work)
1 1/2 tsp	all-purpose flour
1	large head romaine lettuce, washed, dried and ripped in bite-sized pieces
1/2 cup	freshly grated or shaved Parmesan cheese Anchovies (optional)

What would a girl's cookbook be without a winning Caesar salad recipe? A sham and a farce. Thankfully, this book is neither, and with the added touch of Parmesan fricos and homemade croutons and dressing, hail to the ultimate fix for menstrual cravings!

1. To make the croutons, heat olive oil in a large, preferably nonstick frying pan over medium heat. Add crushed garlic and cook, stirring, until golden. Trash the clove, then add bread cubes, stirring to coat with oil. Get them good and toasty. Drain on paper towels and add a few shakes of salt. No noshing.

2. To make the dressing, get out the blender (or a whisk and bowl, or a jar with a lid) and mix together the garlic, egg yolk, lemon juice, lemon zest, W-sauce, sugar, mustard powder, salt and pepper. While blending or whisking, gradually pour in oil until emulsified and yummy. Best made at least a few hours in advance to allow the flavours to meld and develop.

3. To make the fricos, wipe out the pan you used for the croutons. It's really got to be nonstick this time, so get out a different pan if need be. (Sorry. That's an extra pan to wash. I feel awful.) Mix together Parmesan and flour. Heat dry pan on medium-low. Spoon cheese mixture into pan

ET TU, BRVTVS?

in even 2-inch rounds that are as flat as possible. Watch them bubble and melt into golden circles. You've got to do this slowly, frying the grease and liquid out of the cheese. It'll take a few minutes. Remove pan from heat, let cheese calm and cool, then flick each frico out of the pan onto a plate, making sure they don't touch each other. They'll turn crispy and delicate.

TO SERVE:

In a large salad bowl, toss torn lettuce with enough dressing to coat. Add croutons and 1/2 cup Parmesan. Toss it up and dish it out on salad plates, topping each serving with a crisp frico (and a couple of anchovies if you're feeling nasty).

TRIPLE GRILLED CHEESE SANDWICHES:
You Think You Know Grilled Cheese? You Don't Know Jack

—

Serves 4

1	loaf egg bread (a.k.a. challah), sliced
1 tbsp	Dijon mustard (approx)
1/2 lb	old Cheddar, sliced
1	large ripe tomato, thickly sliced
	A few grinds of pepper
12	slices bacon,* cooked crisp
	Margarine for frying (doesn't burn as easily as butter)

A classic grilled cheese sandwich is something that really shouldn't be toyed with—the perfect lunchtime meal or hangover cure. But what if, and I'm just saying if, you used extra-sharp Cheddar and added fresh slices of tomato? And maybe a few pieces of bacon and a smear of Dijon? And how about throwing an extra slice of egg bread in there? Would that appeal to you?

1. Get a slice of bread, smear with mustard. Put a couple of slices of cheese on top and a thick slice of tomato. Grind some pepper on there. Put another slice of bread on top and push down a bit. Give it a smear of mustard, a couple slices of cheese and a few strips of bacon. Put third piece of bread on top. Press down again. Smear top of slice with some margarine.

2. Heat a dollop of margarine in a large nonstick frying pan on medium heat. Place one sandwich, margarine side up, in heated pan. Cook until bottom browns, smooshing down with a spatula a bit. Carefully flip and brown other side too. Cheese should melt, filling should become hot and gooey, knees should weaken. Remove from pan, let cool for a second, then slice on the diagonal.

3. Repeat this process three more times (easiest when done assembly-line style).

TO SERVE:

Ketchup and french fries would make this the perfect comfort meal. (But it might also kill you.)

*SUBSTITUTION ALERT
Veggie bacon in lieu of the real stuff makes this veggie-riffic.

MARINATED JAPANESE VEGETABLES:
Not a Dilly of a Pickle

Serves 6

1 cup	seasoned rice vinegar
1/4 cup	sugar
1/4 cup	water
1/2 tsp	salt
2	large carrots, peeled and sliced
1	medium daikon,* peeled and sliced in half moons
1	cucumber, peeled, seeded (scoop 'em out with a spoon) and sliced in half moons
1	red pepper, diced
1/4 cup	chopped fresh coriander

These ain't your grandma's kosher dills.

1. In a small nonreactive saucepan, bring vinegar, sugar, water and salt to a boil. Pour over prepared veggies in a bowl. Cover and let sit for at least 1 hour. Drain and stir in coriander.

TO SERVE:
A great crunchy side to fish dishes, salads and sandwiches.

*Daikon is a long and lean, cream-coloured radish with a slightly sweet, crisp crunch. It's available at most Asian markets.

LEMON ROASTED POTATOES:
You Say Potato, I Say Lemon

Serves 8

There is no greater comfort food than a dish of steaming hot, crispy-around-the-edges, roasted potatoes. These ones have a citrusy punch that says, "Well hello there! Nice to finally meet you! Have a great day!"

8	Yukon Gold or russet potatoes, peeled and quartered
1/2 cup	extra virgin olive oil
	Juice of 3 lemons (1/2 to 2/3 cup)
1/2 tsp	lemon zest
2 tsp	dried oregano
1 1/2 tsp	sea salt
	Cracked black pepper
1 cup	water

1. Preheat oven to 450°F.
2. In a large ovenproof dish, toss all ingredients together, then pour in water. Bake, uncovered, for 50 minutes to 1 hour, flipping potatoes every so often. When done, the potatoes will be golden brown and crispy on the outside, soft on the inside, with a wallop of lemony excellence.

TO SERVE:
Nice with fish, nice with chicken and salad. A zesty kick in the pants to regular baked or mashed.

DOUBLE-BAKED POTATOES:
Mr. Potato Head, I Love You

—

Serves 4

4	large baking potatoes
1 tsp	oil
1 tsp	kosher salt
1 tbsp	unsalted butter
3/4 cup	warm milk
2 tsp	Dijon mustard
1 tsp	salt
	Cracked pepper to taste
1 cup	bite-sized broccoli florets, partially cooked (micro or boil for 2 minutes)
1 cup	shredded extra-old Cheddar cheese
	Sour cream (optional)

My friend and I were driving to Montreal and made a pit stop at Wendy's. We were amazed to see that the majority of people were chowing down not on their trademark square burgers and chocolaty frosties but rather on big salads, grilled chicken sandwiches and stuffed baked potatoes. Could this be the way of the fast-food future? I also found it touching that smiley retirees dressed in uniforms were walking around pouring coffee refills. Again, could this be the way of the future?

1. Preheat oven to 400°F.
2. Wash and dry potatoes. Poke each with a fork several times, rub with oil and a bit of salt, and bake right on oven rack for 50 minutes or until tender.
3. Slice top 1/4 inch off each potato; scoop out potato innards from potato and caps into a bowl, leaving the potato walls intact. Mash potato in bowl. Stir in butter, warm milk, mustard, salt and pepper until blended and tasty. Place potato skins on a cookie sheet and load mixture into each potato. Top with broccoli and cheese.

4. Bake for 20 minutes or until cheese is bubbly and golden brown.

TO SERVE:

A double-baked potato, a side of sour cream, a little side salad, and you're good to go.

I'M ALL ABOUT OPTIONS

Ditch the broccoli for a topping of chili sprinkled with cheese. Or get fancy and chop up some smoked salmon and mix it with snipped chives, lemon zest and sour cream. For Southwestern flair, mix the innards with shredded Jack cheese, sour cream, pickled jalapeños and green onions.

CRÈME BRÛLÉE THREE WAYS:
Et Tu, Brûlée, Brûlée, Brûlée?

Serves 8

4 cups	whipping cream (yikes!)
1 tsp	vanilla (seeds from a fresh vanilla bean would be even nicer)
8	egg yolks, at room temperature
2/3 cup plus	
1/2 cup	granulated sugar

Crème brûlée needs no introduction. Just a silver spoon and rabid heart.

1. Preheat oven to 300°F.
2. Pour cream into a medium saucepan and over medium heat bring to boiling point, stirring often. Just as a couple of bubbles break the surface, remove from heat. Stir in vanilla (or seeds). Meanwhile, in a large stainless steel bowl, whisk together egg yolks with 2/3 cup sugar until sugar dissolves and mixture is pale and smooth.
3. Put a damp kitchen towel under the bowl to help secure it in place, or have a pal hold the bowl for you. Add a dash of the hot cream to the egg mixture and stir thoroughly. This gets the eggs ready for the shock of the rest of the hot liquid. (Culinary term alert: this is called tempering the eggs.) Whisking continuously, pour the rest of the cream into the egg yolk mixture in a very slow, steady stream, whisking until mixture thickens enough to coat the back of a wooden spoon. If anything bad is going to happen

STOP HITTING ME, YOU HOOLIGAN

(i.e., the eggs scrambling), this is when it's going to happen. (If it does, you'll have to start over. Sorry.) Also, if you let the cream cool down too much before this marrying step, that could also be a problem. In that case, pour some water into the empty cream saucepan, put it over high heat, put the bowl over the pot and whisk the mixture until it thickens.

4. But I digress. Procure a baking dish large enough to hold eight 6-oz ramekins. Place ramekins in baking dish, then using a large measuring cup, fill equally with custard. Using the rinsed-out measuring cup, carefully pour enough hot water down the side of the baking dish until it comes halfway up the ramekins. Do not allow any water to spatter or drip into the custard cups. Bake for 50 minutes to 1 hour or until just set; the centres should jiggle a bit, and you don't want much browning on top. Gently remove custards from water, dry off ramekins, cover with plastic wrap and chill for at least 3 hours or overnight.

5. Cover the top of each chilled ramekin with an even layer of sugar, about 1 tbsp each.

SPECIAL TOOL

You need a blowtorch. You can get either an expensive but sexy little number from a place like Williams-Sonoma or a cheapo but equally useful industrial one from Canadian Tire or a similar store. Tell the service reps what you're using it for and they'll set you up.

Just before serving, so guests can see what a hardass flame-thrower looks like, get out the torch. Fire it up. Don't be scared. One at a time, tilt and turn each ramekin, keeping the fire close to the sugar, using a sweeping motion. Melt the sugar to a dark amber colour, then let cool. (Alternatively, you could turn on the oven broiler to caramelize the sugar, but I haven't had much success with this method.)

TO SERVE:
Get out that silver spoon we talked about earlier. And if you have any other questions, please consult the haiku.

ODE TO CRÈME BRÛLÉE (IN HAIKU)
By Amy Rosen

A crack of the spoon
Burnt sugar glaze exploding
Out oozes heaven

FOR CHOCOLATE BRÛLÉE:
Follow the basic recipe, but stir 8 oz of chopped good-quality milk chocolate in with the cream as it heats up.

FOR FRESH RASPBERRY BRÛLÉE:
Follow the basic recipe, but divide a half pint (1 cup) of washed and well-dried room-temperature raspberries among the ramekins before filling with the custard.

HOW TO IMPRESS BOY TOY *AND* HIS PARENTS:
Easy kudos for the novice chef

You're hip, they're not. You're dating their baby and in no way does this impress them. Thankfully, you're ready to work your mojo. Invite boyfriend's parents over for dinner. Be sure to clean house and tuck away all sex toys, nasty home videos and porn (baby's favourite). Then set a nice table, including flowers, linen napkins and your best Fiestaware. Give them the sophisticated evening I know you can, and soon they'll be calling you "future daughter-in-law." A vast improvement over what they used to call you.

OVEN-ROASTED ARTICHOKE HEARTS WITH PISTACHIO AÏOLI:
Oh, My Nutty Heart

—

Serves 4

14–18	thawed frozen artichoke hearts (or 2 cans, drained and patted dry)
1 tbsp	olive oil
1/2 tsp	sea salt
	Cracked pepper to taste
1 tbsp	minced, fresh parsley

Aïoli:

1/2 cup	Hellmann's mayonnaise (or another primo brand)
1	garlic clove, minced
1 tsp	fresh lemon juice
1 tsp	grated lemon zest
1/4 cup	chopped pistachios

Fresh artichokes are delicious, but also a major pain in the ass. Since I won't bother prepping them, I'm assuming you won't either. But I've come up with a tasty compromise: skip the work of pruning and cleaning and instead buy the frozen or canned (not marinated in oil) ones. Roast them up and side with this engaging sauce. Off you go.

1. Preheat oven to 400°F.
2. In a small baking dish, toss artichoke hearts with oil, salt and pepper. Roast for 20 minutes or until edges just start to brown. Transfer to a bowl and toss with parsley.
3. To make easy aïoli, add mayo, garlic, lemon juice and zest to a small bowl. Stir to combine, then stir in pistachios.

TO SERVE:

Lovely at room temperature, or hot out of the oven. Garnish this special side dish or starter with a thin wedge of lemon and a big dollop of the nutty aïoli.

COCONUT SHRIMP WITH THAI DIPPING SAUCE:
Like Candy Crustaceans

As a university student, I used to have these crunchy critters at my favourite Toronto bar every time I came home for a visit. It was one of those foods I dreamt about while languishing over cold Kraft Dinner. They're crispy and sweet on the outside and moist within. A dose of spicy Thai sauce does them one better.

1. Dip shrimp in egg whites, then roll in coconut. Set aside and let air-dry for a minute.
2. Heat oil over medium-high heat in a large non-stick pan. Cook shrimp, about five at a time, turning once, until coconut is golden brown and tails have turned pink. Drain on paper towel.
3. To make the dipping sauce, stir together the sauce ingredients until sugar dissolves. Taste. Cry.

TO SERVE:

Put the bowl of dipping sauce in the middle of a large plate, pile up a mess of shrimp around it and knock yourself out.

20	shrimp (approx), peeled and deveined, tails left on
2	egg whites, slightly beaten
1 cup	unsweetened shredded coconut
1/2 cup	vegetable oil

Thai Dipping Sauce:

	Juice of 2 small limes
2	large garlic cloves, minced
2	large red hot chilies (such as bird's-eye), seeded and sliced
2 tbsp	fish sauce
1 tbsp	sugar (more or less, depending on taste)
1 tbsp	minced fresh coriander leaves

UDON SALAD WITH SASHIMI TUNA:
Udles of Noodles

Serves 4

1/2 lb	udon noodles (Japanese whole-wheat noodles)
2 cups	julienned vegetables (matchstick-size cuts), including carrots, red pepper, cabbage, snowpeas, resting in ice water
1/4 cup	rice vinegar
2 tbsp	soy sauce
2 tbsp	mirin (see p. 13)
1/2 tsp	finely chopped fresh ginger
1/2 tsp	sesame oil
4 oz	sashimi-grade tuna, thinly sliced
4 tsp	toasted sesame seeds

Crunchy, crisp and zingy; it's like there's a party going on in your mouth and everyone's invited. Even though this healthy noodle dish is a snap to make, be sure to emerge from the kitchen panting and dramatically wiping your brow. It'll taste better.

1. In a medium pot of salted boiling water, cook the noodles until done (follow the package directions and taste for doneness). Drain in a colander and let cool.
2. Drain and pat dry crisp veggies with paper towel.
3. In a small bowl, whisk together the vinegar, soy sauce, mirin, ginger and sesame oil.
4. In your serving bowl, toss the noodles with the dressing, then top with the vegetables and slices of tuna. Sprinkle with sesame seeds.

TO SERVE:

After presenting your gorgeous noodle salad to the table of duly impressed parental units, toss, serve and wait for gushing praise. Then take a moment to assure boyfriend's insecure mom that you're a one-hit wonder.

SHOPPING TIP

When buying fish, look for moist, fleshy pieces that don't smell too fishy. If whole, the fish should have clear eyes, bright red gills and a winning smile. Be sure to eat your fresh fish the day or day after you buy it. No sooner, no later.

SMOKED SALMON SALAD BUNDLES:
Another Type of Bundle of Joy

Serves 4

This salad tosses together easy-to-use field greens spiked with sweet cherry tomatoes, a poppyseed dressing and a sheath of luscious salmon. Better than receiving a ribbon-wrapped Tiffany box (almost).

Poppyseed Dressing:	
1/2 cup	sugar
2 tbsp	poppyseeds
1 tsp	mustard powder
1/2 tsp	salt
1/3 cup	balsamic vinegar
1/2	red onion, minced
2/3	cup vegetable oil
1	bag (4–6 cups) prewashed mixed field greens
1/2 pint	cherry tomatoes or grape tomatoes, cut in half if large
3–5 oz	sliced smoked salmon

1. To make the dressing, to a blender (or to a bowl if you're going the bowl-and-whisk route) add sugar, poppyseeds, mustard powder, salt, vinegar and onion. Gradually add oil, blending until combined. (This makes more than you need for this salad but it will keep in the fridge for a couple of weeks. You've gotta figure, you're making it anyway, make extra.)
2. Just before serving, throw salad greens and tomatoes into a large bowl and drizzle with enough dressing to lightly dress the leaves (goopy salads are passé). Divide salad among four chilled salad plates.

TO SERVE:
Wrap or drape each salad with a strip or two of smoked salmon. We're looking for a fair-sized salad with some height and sex appeal. Make sure everyone has some cherry tomatoes. Now present to your guests the salad as gift.

PANKO-FRIED OYSTERS WITH JAPANESE SPINACH:
So Good, Mama-san

Serves 4

Spinach:

1	bunch fresh spinach, washed meticulously, rough stems cut off
2 tbsp	water
1 tbsp	sugar
1 tsp	lemon zest
1 tsp	soy sauce
1/3 cup	sesame seeds, toasted

Fried Oysters:

12	fresh oysters, shucked (the fishmonger can do this for you if you're using them within a few hours; otherwise, get shucking—see p. 89)
	Salt and pepper
1/2 cup	all-purpose flour
2	eggs, beaten
1 cup	panko* (dry breadcrumbs or crushed cornflakes would do in a pinch)
	Vegetable oil for frying
4 tsp	mayonnaise

*Panko are Japanese breadcrumbs available in Asian food stores and some supermarkets. They're really crunchy, sort of sweet crumbs that make a to-die-for, crisp, light coating.

Your food may be delicious (lord knows, this recipe is good enough), but always remember that great meals boil down to showmanship.

1. Put salted water on to boil in a medium saucepan and when boiling, cook spinach for 1 minute. Drain spinach, rinse in cold water and squeeze it with your hands to remove as much water as possible. Gently squeeze into two cylinders by clenching between two fists, then cut spinach tubes into 2-inch lengths.

2. Stir water, sugar, lemon zest and soy sauce together in a medium bowl until sugar dissolves, then add toasted sesame seeds. Add spinach and toss with dressing. Set aside.

3. Wash the shucked oysters gently but very well to remove any grit, then pat dry on paper towel. Lightly salt and pepper them. In three separate bowls or plates, have ready the flour, beaten eggs and panko. Heat a few inches of oil in a wok or deep skillet to 350°F. (If you don't have a deep-fat thermometer, you'll know it's hot enough when you drop a bit of panko in there and it bubbles.) Dip each oyster in flour, pat off the excess, then dip in egg, then back into flour, back to egg, then give it a final roll and pat in the panko. This little thing will suddenly become a

sizable morsel. Do this for all the oysters, and fry as you go, just a few at a time, cooking them until they're golden brown on both sides, about 40 seconds. Drain cooked oysters on paper towel and sprinkle with a bit of salt.

TO SERVE:

Take four plates and put three hot oysters on each, sided by a lovely mound of the spinach salad. The Japanese love serving these with a dollop of mayo, so feel free. Somehow it works.

POP QUIZ:
READING MEANING INTO YOUR PARTNER'S EATING HABITS

1. If he rests his knife at the 1 o'clock position it means:

☐ He liked the food and is signalling towards a happy finish (and future!).

☐ He didn't enjoy the meal and the knife tip is actually pointing at your aorta in a menacing fashion.

☐ He didn't need the knife for soup.

☐ One o'clock is when lovemaking shall commence—reward for preparing such a rocking meal.

2. If he chews with his mouth open and talks with his mouth full it means:

☐ He's gross.

☐ He's gross, dump him.

☐ He's your dad.

☐ Honestly, if he's not your dad, dump him. He's gross.

3. If he hums with satisfaction while enjoying the food you cooked for him it means:

☐ So sweet! Just like Matt Dillon in *The Flamingo Kid*.

☐ Um, okay. Like, what is he? Two years old?

☐ He may be starting to think of you as mommy. Resolve not to make him pudding anymore.

☐ You're a fabulous girl chef! Who wouldn't hum with delight?

OSSO BUCO WITH BAKED POLENTA:
A Slo-cooked Meallo

Serves 4

1 cup	all-purpose flour (approx)
1 tsp	salt
1/2 tsp	pepper
1 tbsp	butter
1/4 cup	olive oil
4	large veal shanks with marrow bone in centre
1	large onion, chopped
2	garlic cloves, minced
2	large carrots, chopped
2	stalks celery, chopped
1/2 cup	dry white wine or vermouth
1 cup	chicken stock or water (or veal stock if you've got some)
1 cup	canned plum tomatoes, drained and chopped
1 tbsp	tomato paste
Pinch	sugar
2 tsp	lemon zest
1/4 cup	chopped flat-leaf parsley

Polenta:

3/4 cup	all-purpose flour
1/2 cup	fine cornmeal
3/4 tsp	salt
2/3 cup	milk
2 tbsp	unsalted butter, melted
1	egg, beaten
	Cracked pepper to taste

An Italian specialty for filling winter hunger pangs with warmth and evoking the Milan élan. You can skip the polenta if you want, but just so you know, this is a way less finicky recipe than the boiled polenta method. And better tasting too.

1. Mix flour with salt and pepper and set aside. Melt butter with olive oil in a large, heavy frying pan over medium-high heat. Dredge veal shanks in seasoned flour, pat off excess and sear in pan until crispy brown on all sides. Remove from pan and set aside. Drain most of the fat from pan.

2. Sauté the veggies in the remaining fat until lightly browned. Pour in wine and scrape up the brown bits from the bottom. (Culinary-term alert: it's called deglazing the pan.) Stir around for a few minutes, then add the stock, tomatoes, tomato paste and sugar; bring to a boil, then reduce to a simmer. Return the shanks to the pan, cover and simmer on low heat for 2 1/2 hours (or until the meat is falling off the bone), stirring every so often and scraping the bottom. If it gets too dry, add more stock or water. (This step can also be done in a 350°F oven.) Taste for seasoning and adjust accordingly. Just before serving, stir in lemon zest and parsley.

3. Meanwhile, make the polenta. Preheat oven to 350°F. Mix flour, cornmeal and salt together, then stir in milk, melted butter, egg and a few grinds of pepper. Get out a 9-inch pie plate, spray it with nonstick cooking spray and plop the polenta mixture in, spreading it out evenly. Bake for 25 minutes or until the edges start to brown. Cool for five minutes and cut into wedges.

TO SERVE:

A slice of polenta, some veg, a shank and a big thank (you).

GREEN HERBS RISOTTO WITH GARLIC SHRIMP:
We're Here! We're Green! Get Used to It!

Serves 4

Risotto:

2 tbsp	unsalted butter
1 tsp	olive oil
2	garlic cloves, minced
1 cup	minced green onions
1 cup	fresh minced parsley
1 cup	minced spinach
4 cups	vegetable or chicken stock
1 1/2 cups	Arborio rice
1/4 cup	dry white wine or vermouth
1/4 cup	grated or shaved Parmesan cheese (plus extra for garnish)

Shrimp:

1 tbsp	butter
1	garlic clove, minced
8	jumbo shrimp, peeled and deveined, tails left on (for beauty)
	Salt and pepper to taste
	Chopped fresh parsley, for garnish

March down Main Street carrying a placard that says "Dinner at my place. I'm making risotto and shrimp." See what happens.

1. To make the risotto, in a heavy saucepan, melt butter with oil over low heat. Add garlic, green onions, parsley and spinach and cook, stirring occasionally, for 5 minutes. Meanwhile, in another saucepan bring stock to a simmer.

2. Add rice to spinach mixture, stirring to coat all the rice. Add 1 cup warm stock, stir, bring to a boil and let it absorb. Keep adding stock, about 1/2 cup at a time, and stirring, letting the rice absorb the liquid before you add more, until all the stock has been used and the rice is creamy and tender. Stir, stir, stir! From start to finish, this process will take about 25 minutes.

3. Stir in the wine, cheese and maybe a knob of butter if you're feeling naughty. Remove from the heat and keep warm.

4. Now cook the shrimp. In a small frying pan, melt butter over medium-high heat till it's bubbly. Add garlic and cook, stirring, for 30 seconds, then add shrimp and cook until pink on both sides, about 2 minutes. Season with salt and pepper.

TO SERVE:

Dish it up while it's hot. Top each plate of risotto with a couple of shrimp and a shaving of Parmesan. Finish with a sprinkling of fresh parsley and a flourish of pepper grindings.

MARTINIS
For Mama Bear and Papa Bear
Each drink serves 1

Martinis cut the ice like no other cocktail can. But before you mix them up, ask your guests if they like them prepared a specific way. People are surprisingly finicky about their 'tinis.

DRY MARTINI (FOR HIM)
2 oz gin
Splash of dry vermouth
Green olive and lemon twist, for garnish

To a martini shaker two-thirds full of ice cubes, add gin and dry vermouth. Shake briefly, then strain into a chilled martini glass. Serve with a fat green olive and a lemon twist.

SWEET MARTINI (FOR HER)
1 1/2 oz gin
Splash of sweet vermouth
Dash of orange bitters
Maraschino cherry and lemon twist, for garnish

To a martini shaker two-thirds full of ice cubes, add gin, sweet vermouth and orange bitters. Shake briefly, then strain into a chilled martini glass. Serve with a maraschino cherry and a lemon twist.

BEEF TENDERLOIN WITH DRIED CRANBERRY SAUCE:
Showstopping Steer

—

Serves 4–6

2 tsp	finely chopped fresh rosemary
3	garlic cloves, minced
1 tbsp	olive oil, divided
1	beef tenderloin (about 1 1/2 lb)
	Salt and pepper
1/2 cup	dry red wine
1/2 cup	dried cranberries
1 cup	beef broth (bouillon or canned is fine)
1/2 cup	water
1 tsp	cornstarch
3 tbsp	blackcurrant jelly

You Naughty Girl: you like your men young; you can't help it. They're wry and virile and still untainted by the hardships of the world. Besides, New Guy looks great in those jeans. Better still, he's wild for you and your joie de vivre—and you remind him of his mother. Use the best of both worlds to your advantage in one decadent dish. Make this saucy tenderloin, then lovingly tousle his hair and tell him how proud he makes you. New Guy will take care of dessert—a heaping portion of Oedipus Delight. Yummy!

1. Grind rosemary and garlic with the flat side of a knife against your chopping board (or in a mini chopper) to make a paste. Transfer paste to a small bowl and stir in 1 1/2 tsp of the olive oil.
2. Use paper towel to pat tenderloin dry, then rub with rosemary-garlic paste. Season with pepper, cover with plastic wrap and put in fridge for 20 minutes.
3. Preheat oven to 450°F.
4. Heat a cast-iron pan (or heavy ovenproof frying pan) on high heat. Coat hot pan with remaining 1 1/2 tsp oil, season meat with salt, then sear, turning a few times, about 3 minutes on each side. Put pan in oven and roast tenderloin 15 to 20 minutes for medium-rare (a meat

thermometer will read 125°F). Transfer meat to a plate and cover with foil.

5. Add wine and cranberries to pan and deglaze by stirring and scraping up brown bits and letting wine bubble away for a few minutes.

6. In a bowl stir together broth, water and cornstarch. Add to pan and stir for 5 minutes or until sauce thickens further. Whisk in jelly and salt and pepper to taste.

TO SERVE:

Slice luscious tenderloin into 1/2-inch slices and top with sauce. Siding it with braised Brussels sprouts and roasted potatoes makes a perfect meal.

CARAMELIZED MANGO AND BANANA IN PHYLLO PURSES:
It's Impossible to Find Shoes to Match

Serves 4

4 tbsp	unsalted butter
2	large mangoes, peeled and chopped
2	large bananas, sliced in 1/2-inch pieces
1/2 cup	brown sugar
1/2 tsp	vanilla
4	sheets phyllo dough,* thawed and waiting in its waxed paper under a damp tea towel

They say that in cooking, presentation is nine-tenths of the battle. With these crispy pouches stuffed with sweet tropical fruit in a hot caramelly sauce, you'll score a perfect 10 with any culinary judge.

1. In a medium non-stick frying pan, melt 2 tbsp butter over medium heat. Add mangoes and bananas and cook, stirring all around, for 2 minutes. Add sugar and vanilla; cook for another minute or two. With a slotted spoon, transfer the fruit to a bowl.

2. Cook the goop in the pan for another few minutes, stirring, until it begins to get bubbly and caramelly-looking. Toss the fruit back into the pan, take it off the heat, and stir so that everything is uniformly coated. Set aside.

3. Preheat oven to 400°F. Spray a cookie sheet with nonstick cooking spray.

4. Keeping unused phyllo wrapped and under the damp towel, cut one sheet of phyllo lengthwise into four long strips and put back under the damp towel. Then cut a sheet of foil into four 12- by 1-inch strips. These fragile strips will be used to fasten the purses in a decorative fashion.

5. In a small saucepan, or in the microwave, melt the remaining 2 tbsp butter. Place a sheet of phyllo on the counter, carefully brush the whole

thing with some melted butter, then fold in half crosswise to form a rectangle. Now you've got that two-ply thing happening. Brush with more butter, then drop about ¼ cup of the caramel-fruit mixture into the centre. Gather up the edges over the centre and wrap a foil string around the neck of the purse, pinching the foil together to tie it. Take one phyllo strip and carefully tie it around the fastened neck, just below where the foil is holding things together. Keep foil in place. Brush the phyllo string with butter, and give the outside a light brushing as well. Transfer the purse to the cookie sheet and repeat for the remaining three purses.

5. Bake for 10 to 12 minutes or until golden brown. Allow to cool for a bit, then gently remove foil string.

TO SERVE:

Perfect on its own, or side it with a scoop of vanilla ice cream or mango sorbet. And wouldn't a sprig of mint be pretty?

*Phyllo is a prepared paper-thin dough that can be found in the freezer section of most supermarkets. Sometimes it's spelled filo. Same difference.

BAKING TIP
Change the fruit filling. McDonald's does it. Why can't you?

IF IT AIN'T BROKE, DON'T FIX IT:
Retro one-pot meals

This isn't about "set it and forget it," but these recipes are almost as easy as huckster Ron Popeil's TV pitch (although no special electronic equipment or four easy-pay installments will be needed here). Make-ahead or à la minute: either way you slice and dice it, you'll be pleasing the taste buds—and cutting down on dishwashing duties.

FRENCH ONION SOUP:
Waiter, There's Some Deliciousness in My Soup

—

Serves 6

1/4 cup	unsalted butter
6	large onions, sliced
2	garlic cloves, sliced
1/2 cup	dry red wine
1/4 cup	brandy
6 cups	canned low-sodium beef broth
1	bay leaf
2 tsp	Dijon mustard
	Salt and pepper to taste
Pinch	sugar

Topping:

4	thick baguette slices, toasted
2 cups	shredded Gruyère cheese

A wintertime family favourite from a '70s childhood spent at the cottage. Caesar salad, this Parisian soup, a roaring fire and a rousing game of charades.

1. Melt butter in a large, heavy saucepan over medium heat. Add onions and garlic and cook, stirring freqeuntly, until tender and very browned, about 50 minutes. (Sure, it takes a while, but the caramelization of the onions is key to the recipe, and you don't have to stir constantly. Go check your e-mail.) When nice and caramelized, stir in wine and brandy; simmer until liquid is reduced to almost nothing, about 3 minutes. Stir in broth, bay leaf and mustard, give a good stir, scraping up the bottom bits. Simmer 20 minutes. Season with salt and pepper and a pinch of sugar if need be.

2. Preheat broiler. Ladle soup into onion soup bowls (or ovenproof regular soup bowls), set on a cookie sheet. Top each bowl with a slice of toast and grated cheese. Broil till top bubbles and browns.

TO SERVE:

Put a napkin on a plate and, using oven mitts, put a bowl on each plate, sided by a big soupspoon. Warn your guests that the bowls are extremely hot. Then watch everyone burn his or her tongue on molten cheese. Priceless.

PASSING THOUGHT

When sliced onions are cooked low and slow, they melt down and are rendered sweet like nobody's business. Plain rendered cooking onions are actually the best variety to use for the soup, as they add a nice depth of flavour. Finally—a bargain! You can always use fancier Vidalias (naturally sweeter by about 7%) or Spanish varietals, but the extra cost gets lost in the cooking.

LAMB STEW WITH ROSEMARY DUMPLINGS:
The Stew That Eats Like a Stew

—

Serves 4–6

Stew:

2 lb	stewing lamb, cut in 2-inch cubes
2 tbsp	all-purpose flour
	Salt and pepper to taste
Pinch	cayenne
2 tbsp	vegetable oil
2	onions, chopped
3	shallots, chopped
2 tbsp	tomato paste
Pinch	sugar
1/2 cup	water
1 cup	red wine
3	large carrots, cut in 1-inch pieces
1/2 cup	frozen peas

Dumplings:

1 1/2 cups	all-purpose flour
2 tsp	baking powder
1/2 tsp	salt
	Cracked pepper to taste
1/2 tsp	crumbled dried rosemary
3 tbsp	vegetable shortening
3/4 cup	water (approx)

Three words: STEW IS BACK. (Big time.)

1. Trim gristle and excess fat off lamb cubes. Mix flour with salt, pepper and cayenne. Toss lamb in flour mixture, then pat off the excess.

2. In your biggest pot, heat vegetable oil over high heat. Working in batches and without crowding the pot, toss in cubes of meat, turning them every so often so that they brown well on all sides; remove them as they're cooked. Once all the meat is browned, reduce the heat to medium and return the cooked meat to the pot. Toss in the onions and shallots and let them sweat for a couple of minutes with the meat. Add the tomato paste and sugar. Stir in the water and scrape up the good browned bits from the bottom of the pot. Cook for 5 minutes, then stir in the wine and bring to a boil. Taste for seasoning, add more salt and pepper if need be.

3. Reduce heat to a low simmer, cover the pot and cook for 90 minutes, stirring about every 20 minutes. Grab a bite to test/taste. A knife should glide through the meat. Toss in the carrots and cook for 20 more minutes. If the stew is getting a little dry, add a bit more water.

4. Meanwhile, let's make the dumplings. In a bowl, mix together flour, baking powder, salt, pepper

and rosemary. Add the shortening, working it in with a fork so that it's all broken down and the mixture looks grainy. Slowly stir in the water until the dough is light but solid and can be easily dropped from a spoon.

5. Give the stew a stir, add the peas, then let the aroma momentarily take you away. Using a wet soupspoon, scoop up mounds of dumpling dough and drop them on the stew, spacing them out around the perimeter first, then working your way in. Do not stir! Put on the lid (no peeking) and don't lift it again for 20 minutes, a.k.a. dinnertime.

TO SERVE:

Dish it out in hearty heapings, giving everyone a couple of dumplings on top. And toss some parsley on there if you're feeling fancy.

PASSING THOUGHT

Stew tastes even better the next day. Same goes for pizza, spaghetti—and Bloody Marys.

ROASTED BEEF BRISKET:
A Jewish Girl's Rite of Passage

Serves 10

1	brisket (about 5 lb)
1 cup	Coca-Cola (not diet, not lemon-flavoured, just Classic, please)
1 cup	apricot jam
1/2 cup	tomato sauce
1	packet onion soup mix
1 tsp	ground ginger
1 tsp	kosher salt
	Cracked pepper to taste

You don't know exactly when it happens—some time after your bat mitzvah but a bit before you marry. You'll eat at someone's house, they'll serve up brisket, and you'll ask for and receive the recipe. Soon after, it becomes your own. As one New York socialite once said to another: "You can never be too rich, too thin, or have too many brisket recipes." Here's a classic, passed on from one friend to another. That's me to you. Because I do consider us friends by now. (Just don't call me; I'm unlisted.)

1. Put brisket in a roasting pan. Combine Coca-Cola, jam, tomato sauce, soup mix, ginger, salt and pepper. Pour over brisket, cover with foil and refrigerate overnight.
2. Good morning! Preheat oven to 325°F. Cook brisket, covered with foil, for about 3 hours. Uncover and cook for another 30 minutes. Let it cool, then refrigerate (this aids in slicing). When cooled, remove from sauce (but reserve sauce in pan) and slice thinly against the grain.
3. About a half hour before you're ready to serve it, preheat oven to 325°F again. Cover the brisket in the roasting pan with the sauce, spooning it over a bit, and heat for 20 to 30 minutes.

Chicken soup, salad, gefilte fish, potato kugel, carrot tzimmes and some nice brisket. Eat. Eat! You're all skin and bones.

TIN FOIL:
TOP FIVE USES FOR THE WORLD'S
MOST USEFUL WRAP
1. Better TV reception.
2. Nuclear-strength tanning surface.
3. Pinches into a glittery ball,
   Patches' favourite cat toy.
4. Makeshift mirror (shiny side).
5. More flattering makeshift
   mirror (dull side).

ROASTED ROOT VEGETABLES WITH BALSAMIC VINAIGRETTE:
Fruits of the Earth

Serves 6

1	can (15 oz) baby beets, drained
2	medium sweet potatoes, peeled and cut in 1-inch cubes
10	baby potatoes
3	large carrots, peeled and cut in 1-inch chunks
2	large parsnips, peeled and cut in 1-inch chunks
6	shallots, peeled
2 tbsp plus 2 tsp	olive oil
1/2 tsp	dried oregano
1/2 tsp	salt
1/4 tsp	black pepper
2 tbsp	balsamic vinegar
1/2 tsp	freshly grated lemon zest
	Salt and pepper to taste

Peel some veggies, chop them up, pop them in the oven and forget about them. For about an hour. After they're all caramelized and smelling like the celestial skies, toss them with the zingy vinaigrette, then go kiss your greengrocer.

1. Preheat oven to 450°F.
2. Throw the prepared vegetables into a roasting pan, then drizzle everything with 2 tbsp olive oil, the oregano, salt and pepper. Toss the whole mess together so that every bit is coated with oil and seasonings. Roast, stirring every 15 minutes or so, until the vegetables are tender and caramelized, which will take 45 to 50 minutes.
3. In a small bowl, whisk together remaining 2 tsp olive oil, vinegar and lemon zest. Throw in a pinch of salt and pepper to taste. Pour the vinaigrette over the cooked veggies and toss to coat.

TO SERVE:

A toothsome side dish for roasted meats. In fact, they're so good you'll probably opt to skip the meat altogether and just tuck into the roasted veggie goodness.

TINY ROASTED POTATOES WITH SAGE BUTTER:
Baby Potatoes All Grown Up

Remember that hilariously pathetic scene in *Swingers*, when Jon Favreau's character left, like, 19 messages on his ex-girlfriend's answering machine? Classic. These potatoes are also a classic-in-the-making, and funny too. Not so much ha-ha funny as yum-yum funny.

1/4 cup	unsalted butter
1 tbsp	crumbled dried sage
3 lb	new potatoes, white or red or a combo
1 tsp	kosher salt
	Cracked pepper

1. Preheat oven to 375° F.
2. Melt butter with sage in a small saucepan to infuse the sage flavour into the butter. Let simmer for a few minutes.
3. Roll potatoes into a roasting pan or onto a couple of cookie sheets. Drizzle with sage butter, sprinkle with salt and pepper and toss to coat evenly. Bake for about 40 minutes, or until golden on the outside and soft on the inside.

TO SERVE:

What are you looking for, operating instructions? They're potatoes!

KITCHEN HINT
Keep potatoes and other root vegetables in a dark, cool place, like under the kitchen sink. They'll stay daisy-fresh even longer when stored in paper bags.

CLASSIC MEAT LASAGNA:
For Goodfellas and Hungry Fellas

Serves 8

2 tbsp	olive oil
2	garlic cloves, minced
1	onion, chopped
3/4 lb	lean ground beef, cooked until browned (about 5 minutes), fat drained
1	can (28 oz) whole plum tomatoes, drained and chopped
1	can (28 oz) crushed plum tomatoes
1 cup	dry red wine
2 tsp	dried oregano
1/4 cup	chopped fresh basil
1/2 tsp	sugar
1/2 tsp	salt
1/4 tsp	cracked black pepper
1/4 tsp	chili flakes
1	egg
1	pkg (10 oz) frozen spinach, thawed, squeezed of excess water and chopped
1 cup	ricotta cheese
1/2 cup	grated Parmesan cheese
10	oven-ready lasagna noodles (approx)
2 cups	shredded mozzarella cheese

Hearty and cheesy, this big pan of gooey glory ain't for patsies. But it's so easy that I'm going to have to ask you to make your own sauce, just so that you can say you actually had an active hand in preparing something this impressive. Bada-bing!

1. Make the sauce. This entails putting a medium saucepan on the stove, heating up the olive oil over medium heat, adding garlic and onions and cooking them for a couple of minutes, stirring to make sure they don't burn. Then stir in the cooked ground beef, drained tomatoes, crushed tomatoes, wine, oregano, basil, sugar, salt, pepper and chili flakes. Simmer over medium-low heat for an hour or so, stirring every so often. Taste and adjust seasonings. More salt? Another pinch of sugar? Spice it up? Your sauce, your choice. (You could also skip this step altogether and just buy a couple of jars of tomato sauce. But didn't I just tell you it was easy?)

2. In a bowl, beat the egg. Add spinach, ricotta cheese and Parmesan cheese. Stir it up.

3. Now for the assembly. Preheat oven to 350°F. Get out a large ovenproof baking dish, preferably 13 by 9 inches, but do what you can. Spray with cooking spray.

4. Spread a third of the hot tomato sauce evenly across the bottom of the pan. Layer lasagna noodles (about five) over the sauce so that they overlap slightly and completely cover the sauce, making, in essence, a noodle barrier. Spread some more sauce on the noodles to coat, then spread spinach mixture evenly over this layer. Top with another solid layer of lasagna noodles, then remaining sauce. Sprinkle a thick coating of mozzarella on top.

5. Bake, uncovered, until hot and bubbly, 30 to 40 minutes. Let stand for at least 10 minutes before slicing or it will ooze all over the place and you'll be forced to slap your forehead and exclaim "Mamma mia!"

TO SERVE:

Big even squares are the way to go here. A perfect meal when sided by Caesar salad (p. 40) and garlic bread (p. 78).

DOUBLE-ROASTED GARLIC BREAD:
Twice the Vampire-fighting Power

Serves 8

1	head garlic
1 tsp	olive oil
1 cup	unsalted butter, at room temperature
2 tbsp	finely chopped fresh parsley
2	garlic cloves, minced
1/4 tsp	salt
	Cracked pepper
1	baguette or Italian loaf

As long as everyone's eating it, you'll be fine.

1. Preheat oven to 350°F.
2. Lop about 3/4 inch off the top of the whole garlic bulb. Place decapitated head on a piece of foil, drizzle with olive oil, wrap foil around garlic to encase and seal, then roast for 40 to 50 minutes or until it's soft. Allow to cool, then squeeze garlic into a bowl.
3. Raise oven temperature to 450°F. To the bowl of roasted garlic, add the butter, parsley, minced garlic, salt and pepper. Stir to combine.
4. Slice baguette in even slices without cutting through the bottom crust. (This will hold the bread together and make for easier baking and ceremonial tearing later on.) Slather one side of each slice with butter mixture. Don't be shy, we're all friends here.
5. Wrap in foil and bake until toasty and smelling like garlic heaven, 15 to 20 minutes.

TO SERVE:

Tear and eat. (Best when dipped in lasagna sauce.)

CHEESE FONDUE:
Whereby It's Acceptable to Eat a Bowl of Melted Cheese

Serves 4

Wine and fire and pointy sticks: Hear ye, hear ye! The molten cheese approaches! Catapult the bread cubes over the moat of blanched roots and greenery! Darkness is well nigh and the Royals must be fed!

1. Pour wine into a medium saucepan and heat over medium heat. Gradually add cheeses a handful at a time, stirring constantly until all cheese is melted.
2. Stir together cornstarch and kirsch. Stir into cheese mixture, stirring continuously with a wooden spoon until mixture is smooth and glossy and all is right with the world. Do not let it boil.

TO SERVE:

Arrange prepared bread and veg on a platter. Pour cheese sauce into a fondue pot and light the flame underneath to keep fondue warm. Using fondue forks, skewer bread and veggies and dip into bubbly fondue. You can double-dip as much as you want, but just be mindful not to actually drool into the pot.

1 1/2 cups	Chardonnay
3/4 lb	Gruyère cheese, shredded
3/4 lb	Emmenthal cheese, shredded
1 tsp	cornstarch
1 tbsp	kirsch or brandy
1	baguette, cut in thick slices and each slice quartered
1 cup	broccoli florets, blanched
1 cup	carrot, cut in bite-sized pieces and blanched
1 1/2 cups	red potatoes, cut in half or quarters, boiled until cooked

REAL CHOCOLATE PUDDIN':
It's National Lick-the-Spoon Day!

Serves 6

2 cups	2% milk
3 tbsp	cornstarch
3/4 cup	sugar
1/2 cup	cocoa powder
	Pinch salt
1/2 cup	hot water
1 cup	half-and-half cream
1 tsp	vanilla
6 oz	milk chocolate, chopped

Childhood never tasted *this* good.

1. Heat 1/2 cup of the milk. Whisk in cornstarch and set aside.

2. In a large saucepan combine sugar, cocoa and salt. Whisk in water until there are no visible lumps. Bring to a boil, then simmer for several minutes, stirring constantly until everything is dissolved and uniformly chocolatey-looking.

3. Pour in the rest of the milk and the cream. Give the reserved cornstarch mixture a stir and add to the pot. Give 'er a big old stir, bring to a boil, lower heat to medium-low and keep on stirring until pudding thickens, 5 to 7 minutes.

4. Take pot off of heat and stir in vanilla and chopped chocolate until smooth.

5. Pour pudding into six 6-oz ramekins and let sit at room temperature for a bit.

TO SERVE:

You can either cover the puddings with plastic wrap and let them chill in the fridge for a few hours before serving or eat them warm off the counter. My favourite is letting them cool in the fridge without plastic wrap so that they form a thick, delicious scum, to be peeled off the top and eaten in one bite. Mmm, pudding scum.

FIZZY RUM PUNCH:
An Elmore Leonard Classic

Serves 8–10

Take a big punch bowl—steal it from your parents if you have to. Add sliced fruit. Spike it with rum. Stir. Roll film.

1. Half an hour before serving, mix all the ingredients (except ice) together in a big bowl (preferably a punch bowl). Add the ice right before your guests arrive.

TO SERVE:
You don't need me to tell you what to do.

1	can (12 oz) frozen concentrated orange juice (still frozen)
1	quart orange sherbet, softened
1/2 cup	maraschino cherries with their juice
4 cups	ginger ale
1 1/4 cups	white rum
	Juice of 3 limes
1	lime, thinly sliced
3	seedless oranges, thinly sliced
2	trays of ice

I'M NOT FRENCH, BUT JERRY LOVES MY COOKING:

Classic bistro fare

They smoke too much, drink too much and more often than not, don't shower enough. They're rude to tourists, they let their dogs eat with them in restaurants and they're lazy and arrogant. But you've got to hand it to them—the French know good food. So all is forgiven. I love you, Pierre! Call me!

VICHYSSOISE:
Soup Be Chillin'

___

Serves 4–6

2 tbsp	unsalted butter
2	medium onions, sliced (French tradition calls for the use of leeks, but they're dirty and can be difficult to clean. Forgive me.)
5	medium potatoes, peeled and thinly sliced
4 cups	vegetable stock
1 cup	milk
1 cup	whipping cream
	Salt and pepper to taste
	Snipped chives (optional)

COOKING TIP

Be sure to make the soup several hours before you plan on serving it so that you and it have ample time to chill out, if you know what I mean.

STYLE TIP

Why not throw on a smart outfit to match your chic dish? Dress head to toe in summer whites (can't go wrong with linen), then top off the look with a jaunty green beret. There's always room for a bit of French flair.

When I was a kid attending summer sleepover camp, my brothers and I always looked forward to visitor's day because it meant our parents would be carting a big Tupperware container full of icy vichyssoise. It was our tradition. While other "normal" families devoured buckets of Kentucky Fried chicken and smoked meat sandwiches, we sipped our swanky cold soup and nibbled party sandwiches. It was a bit of an embarrassment. An embarrassment of riches.

1. In a large saucepan, melt butter over medium heat. Add onions and cook for 10 minutes or until very soft. Stir often, making sure they don't brown. Add potatoes and stock. Cover and simmer over medium-low heat for 30 minutes.

2. Turn off the heat, and using a hand blender, purée the contents of the pot in the pot. (Or purée in batches in a blender.) Stir in the milk, cream, salt and pepper.

3. Put in the fridge to chill for at least 3 hours. Once the soup is cold, you may want to adjust the seasoning by adding more salt or pepper.

TO SERVE:

This soup is perfect on its own, majestic in its stark whiteness, or better still, topped with freshly snipped chives.

ROASTED ASPARAGUS POLONAISE:
Jack and the Magic Green Stalks

—

Serves 8

Fresh asparagus is a rite of spring, even though now it's available year round. And remember, when you go to the bathroom after eating this, don't be alarmed. And if you don't know what I'm talking about, this is none of your business.

2 lb	thin asparagus, bottom ends snapped off where they naturally break
1 tbsp	olive oil
1/2 tsp	sea salt
	Cracked pepper to taste
1/4 cup	unsalted butter
1/4 cup	fresh breadcrumbs, toasted
2	hard-cooked eggs, grated on a cheese grater
2 tbsp	minced fresh parsley
	Salt and pepper to taste

1. Preheat oven to 500°F.
2. Toss asparagus with oil, salt and pepper. Spread out on a cookie sheet (use two if too crowded) and roast for 8 to 10 minutes or until lightly golden, shaking pan to roll asparagus over halfway through. Lay asparagus in a serving dish.
3. To make the classic polonaise topping, melt butter in a small saucepan, let it bubble, then add breadcrumbs. Remove from heat and stir in eggs, parsley and salt and pepper to taste.

TO SERVE:

Line the lovely little stalks up in a nice serving dish so that all heads face north (did you know there are special asparagus-centric serving vessels? Pick one up at a yard sale), then pour on hot topping to cover. Also good at room temp.

WILD MUSHROOM SOUP WITH PASTRY CAPS:
Trippin' Soupe du Jour

—

Serves 6

1 oz	dried porcini mushrooms
2 tbsp	unsalted butter
1/2 cup	finely chopped shallots
2	garlic cloves, minced
3 cups	chopped button mushrooms
1/2 tsp	salt
	Cracked pepper to taste
1/2 cup	dry sherry
4 cups	vegetable stock
1/2 cup	whipping cream
2 tbsp	snipped chives

Pastry Caps:

1	14-oz pkg frozen puff pastry (2 blocks), thawed
1	egg, beaten with 1 tsp water (a.k.a. egg wash)

This is a gourmet soup with a soothing texture, sly hits of exotic porcini mushrooms, a spiking of sherry and a dash of cream. The puff pastry cap could be seen as overkill, but who doesn't like to be dazzled?

1. Place porcini in a bowl, cover with boiling water and let stand until softened, about 30 minutes. Remove mushrooms but reserve the soaking liquid (full of flavour!). Gently squeeze excess water from the mushrooms and coarsely chop them.

2. Melt butter in a large saucepan over medium-high heat. Add shallots and sauté for a few minutes, then add garlic, porcini, button mushrooms, salt and pepper. Cook for another fiver. Add sherry and boil until almost all liquid evaporates, then pour in reserved 'shroom soaking liquid and stock, taking care not to include any grit. Simmer for 10 minutes, taste for seasoning, remove from heat and purée with a hand blender, leaving some chunks of 'shrooms intact. Stir in cream and chives, then ladle soup into six onion soup bowls (widely available at discount stores and yard sales).

3. Now it's time to get really fancy. Preheat oven to 400°F. To prepare the puff pastry caps, on a lightly floured surface roll out one block puff pastry into a 12-inch square and cut out four

circles that are about 3/4 inch larger than the diameter of the bowls. Roll out second block and cut out two more rounds. Brush excess flour off rounds. Brush a 1/2-inch-wide border of egg wash around pastry edges and flip rounds over soup bowls, carefully stretching 1/2 inch down side and pressing to seal (egg wash = glue). When all bowls are pastry capped, brush tops with remaining egg wash.

4. Arrange soup bowls on a large cookie sheet and bake until pastry is puffed and golden, 12 to 15 minutes.

TO SERVE:

Oy, if your mother could see you now. Place each crisp-capped bowl on top of a napkin on a salad plate and warn eager eaters that the bowls are extremely hot as they have just come out of the oven. Then watch as each person touches his or her bowl just to see *how* hot. It's human nature.

OYSTER SHOTS:
So Seductive You Might as Well Serve Them Naked

Makes 6

6	fresh oysters, shucked
1	small shallot, minced
2 tbsp	red wine vinegar
Dash	Tabasco sauce
6 oz	ice-cold vodka of choice

Place aphrodisiacs in shot glasses. Stir to combine. Remove panties. Drink.

1. Shuck oysters if your fishmonger didn't do it for you (see sidebar on shucking). Mix together shallot, vinegar and Tabasco. Plop a fat oyster into each of six chilled vodka glasses, spoon on some shallot-vinegar mixture (a.k.a. mignonette sauce) and pour 1 oz vodka over each (I wouldn't say no to free-pouring).

TO SERVE:
If you need me to tell you what to do, I guess I just don't know you as well as I thought I did.

I took an oyster-shucking class at my favourite Toronto bivalve bistro one sunny Saturday. John, our instructor, walked us through the history of the oyster in North America whilst we sipped pints of Guinness perhaps a bit too early in the morn. This is what I learned. Bivalves have two shells, and there are two ways to open them: by heat (but that would entail cooking them) or by prying them open. Prying them open keeps the animal within alive and succulent. Bigger oysters are usually better oysters. They should have an even shape, a flat top and a deep rounded cup (the bottom shell). They should be heavy for their size, contain lots of clear liquid, and the meat of the oyster should be oyster-coloured (creamy) with some dark brown tinges (the organs). If there's no liquid and the oyster has a green tinge to it, ditch it. Always smell an oyster before eating it. If you don't and something bad happens, you've only got yourself to blame.

This is how to shuck an oyster: You must pop the hinge, cut the abductor muscle—and then it's slurping time. Place oyster cup side down (the lid is always smaller than the bottom) on a kitchen cloth. Find the tiny space in the hinge of the oyster (at the top at the slender end). Holding the oyster securely with the cloth, slide the tip of a shucking knife into the hinge, and using a pushing and twisting motion, pop that hinge. Once the hinge is popped, use the knife edge to pry the shell open. Work the knife under the tough tendon-like abductor muscle and cut the top and bottom. Honestly, it's easier than it sounds.

BRANDY CHICKEN LIVER CROSTINI:
Foxy Faux Foie Gras

—

Serves 6

1 lb	chicken livers
1/4 cup	all-purpose flour
1/2 tsp	sea salt
	Cracked pepper
1 tbsp	olive oil
2	shallots, minced
1/4 cup	brandy
1/4 cup	whipping cream
2 tsp	crumbled dried sage
1 tbsp	unsalted butter
1 tbsp	chopped fresh parsley
1	baguette, sliced and toasted
	Minced red onion, for garnish (optional)

Want to impress your guests without spending the big bucks? For the same buttery texture at a fraction of the cost, make a fricassee of chicken livers (in lieu of fattened duck or goose liver) enlivened by decadent additions. Your gourmand pals will be none the wiser.

1. Rinse and pat dry the chicken livers. Remove any fat or tendon-like material, then slice each liver in half. Add salt and pepper to flour and dredge livers in seasoned flour. Pat off excess flour.

2. Heat oil in a large frying pan on medium-high heat and sauté shallots until soft. Toss in chicken livers and sauté for a few minutes. Add brandy, stir around for a minute, then add cream and sage. Bring to a boil, reduce heat and simmer for a couple of minutes until sauce thickens a titch. Stir in butter to finish the sauce, then toss in parsley. Taste and season with extra salt and pepper if need be.

TO SERVE:

Top toasted baguette slices with foie gras (wink-wink) mixture and sprinkle with some minced red onion for colour and a bit of bite. It's a cross between a ritzy foie gras appetizer and a chopped liver and schmaltz sandwich. Ooh la la oy vey!

THREE DISTINCTLY FRENCH LIBATIONS:
Pour les Parties Fantastiques

—

Each drink serves 1

They may be too damn romantic, but the French know how to mix a nice cocktail.

PARIS OPERA SPECIAL

Stir together in a highball glass with ice.

1 1/2 oz	fresh grapefruit juice
1 1/2 oz	blue curaçao
1 oz	white rum

CHAMPAGNE COCKTAIL

Pour brandy into a champagne glass and fill the glass to the three-quarters point with champagne. Rub rim with orange peel and discard.

1 oz	brandy
4 oz	icy cold champagne
	Orange peel

LE MANS

Add the Cointreau and vodka to a highball glass. Add soda water to taste and drop in the lemon twist.

2 oz	Cointreau
1 oz	chilled vodka
	Soda water
	Lemon twist

TRÈS BIEN, ENCORE!

ROAST LEG OF LAMB WITH FRESH MINT SAUCE:
You'll Be Counting Juicy Bites in Your Dreams

—

Serves 6–8

1	bone-in leg of lamb (5–6 lb)
10	garlic cloves, cut in slivers
1 tbsp	olive oil
	Juice of 1 lemon
2 tsp	chopped fresh rosemary
1 tsp	kosher salt
	Freshly ground black pepper

Mint Sauce:

1/4 cup	chopped mint leaves
1/4 cup	sugar
1/2 cup	white vinegar
1/4 cup	boiling water

A no-hassle, classic combo of mint and lamb. Ditch the gloopy jelly for this tingly, fresh, updated sauce.

1. Preheat oven to 450°F.
2. Remove most of visible fat from the lamb leg. Make little slits in meat with a sharp knife and insert a sliver of garlic into each slit. (I'm going to be honest with you: this task is a little gruesome, as you may have to use your finger to make the slits large enough. Consider yourself warned.)
3. Place lamb on a wire rack in a roasting pan. Rub with olive oil, pour lemon juice over it and season with rosemary, salt and pepper. Roast for 20 minutes. Turn oven down to 400°F and continue roasting for 50 to 60 minutes for medium-rare. A meat thermometer plunged into the thickest part of the roast (but not touching the bone) should read about 150°F. Let lamb rest, tented with foil, for 15 minutes before carving.
4. For the mint sauce, to a blender add mint, sugar, vinegar and boiling water. Blend together, taste and adjust seasoning if need be, then heat and serve.

TO SERVE:

Present the stunning leg of lamb whole, on a rustic wooden chopping board, and start carving. Pour mint sauce into a gravy dish and have everyone help themselves. Roasted root veggies (p. 74) are the perfect side.

FRESH VERSUS FROZEN

Do you honestly think ice-hard sacks of shrink-wrapped lamb from the supermarket convey the mien of "juicy succulence"? When I'm looking for the nicest cuts, I go to my local butcher. Just like when I want the best bread, I go to the bakery. Candlesticks? Well, you get the point. When in doubt, fresh is best.

FLANK STEAK WITH SHORT-CUT HOLLANDAISE:
Delicious 101

Serves 4

1	flank steak (about 1 1/2 lb and 3/4 inch thick), at room temperature
1 tbsp	olive oil
	Kosher salt and cracked pepper

Hollandaise Sauce:

2	egg yolks
2 tbsp	fresh lemon juice
1/4 tsp	salt
1/2 cup	ice-cold unsalted butter, cut into pats
	Cracked pepper

An inexpensive but tender cut of steak with a decadent sauce. This dish is the yin and yang of the meat world.

1. Rub the flank steak with olive oil and season both sides generously with salt and pepper. Preheat a BBQ or grill pan to medium heat, and grill steak, flipping halfway through cooking time, for 8 to 10 minutes for medium-rare, which is as it should be (this will take longer if your steak is thicker). Set aside to rest for 5 minutes.

2. While the meat rests, make the hollandaise sauce. Get out a saucepan and a stainless steel bowl that can rest on top of the saucepan. Have a larger bowl filled with ice water waiting on the side. Fill the pot halfway with water (make sure the water won't touch the bottom of the bowl) and bring to a simmer. In the bowl, lightly beat the egg yolks, then whisk in the lemon juice and salt. Place the bowl over simmering water—don't let the water boil—and whisk constantly while gradually adding cubes of butter. Whisk until sauce has the consistency of thick gravy. If the eggs start to seize and scramble, immediately plunge the bowl into the icy water. Alternatively, plop in a bunch of cold butter cubes and whisk like your life depends on it. This should save the sauce. If it looks a bit grainy just beat it like mad;

it should smooth out. If it doesn't you're going to have to start from scratch. (I'm sorry. Things happen. Live and learn.) Remove bowl from pot and add pepper to taste.

TO SERVE:
Slice steak across the grain into 1/2-inch slices and serve with a drizzle of buttery hollandaise. A little goes a long way. A fresh, crisp salad and crusty bread complete the deed.

ROAST CHICKEN WITH COGNAC GRAVY:
This Bird's Going Out in Style

Serves 6

1	roasting chicken, 4 1/2–7 lbs.
2 tbsp	olive oil
1 tsp	coarse kosher salt (approx)
	Cracked pepper

Cognac Gravy:

1/4 cup	cognac or brandy
1 cup	good chicken stock
2 tbsp	chopped fresh parsley
1 tsp	Dijon mustard

After the age-old chicken-and-egg question comes, "How does one make the perfect roast chicken?" I did the research, and this recipe takes its cues from Julia Child's famous bird recipe, coupled with pointers from the food scientist nerds at America's Test Kitchen. Roasting a chicken couldn't be easier, unless you opt to pick one up at the supermarket in one of those ingenious paper/foil bags, thereby skipping the hassle of making your own. But this mouth-watering combo of chicken and liquor can't be duplicated by any supermarket. And it's actually really easy.

1. Preheat oven to 450°F.
2. Remove nasty bag of giblets, neck and such from the chicken cavity and pitch it (unless you plan on eating them on another occasion or making a stock, in which case, good for you! Freeze them). Cut off excess skin and fat, rinse the chicken, pat dry and rub with oil. Sprinkle with coarse salt and pepper and massage it all in.
3. Place the chicken breast side up on a wire rack in a roasting pan, tucking in legs and wings. Roast, uncovered, for 15 minutes. Carefully turn chicken on its side and roast another 10 minutes. (The turning part is a bit of a balancing act; if you truss the chicken with string beforehand it adds stability. Either way is fine though.) Baste with

drippings, then turn her on the other side for another 10 minutes. Baste again. (Add a bit of water to the pan if there's not enough fat to baste with.) Reduce the heat to 350°F, turn chicken breast side up again and roast until a meat thermometer stuck into the meaty part of a leg (without touching the bone) registers 170°F, the joints feel loose and the juices run clear. General rule of thumb is about 1 hour of cooking for a 3-lb chicky and an extra 10 minutes for each additional pound. Remove chicken from pan and set aside on a cutting board, tented with foil, for 15 minutes.

4. Tilt roasting pan and spoon off as much fat as you can, reserving dark drippings in the pan. Put pan over high heat on the stove. Stir in cognac and chicken stock, stirring to dislodge all the crispy bottom bits and letting the sauce reduce. Boil and stir until liquid is syrup-like. Strain if you want, or leave as is for more rustic appeal. Stir in parsley and mustard and taste for seasoning.

TO SERVE:

Present your chicken on a large wooden cutting board, and let someone who knows what they're doing carve it up at the table. This could, in fact, be you. Side with a sauceboat of the cognac gravy.

DADDY'S LITTLE GIRL IS ALL GROWN UP
How to Carve a Bird

What was once the domain of the man of the house and his carving knife is now the terrain of the goodtime gal and her stilettos. Not that you're going to use your heels to carve the chicken or turkey. But you are going to look good doing it. Here's what to do.

1. A 9-inch steel carving knife and matching fork are the ideal utensils for this task, but if you're not married and, hence, did not receive these implements as part of your wedding registry, do not fret. Any big sharp blade will do.

2. Jab a big fork into the bird, towards the end of the breastbone. This will steady it. Using the point of the knife, cut the joint that holds the wing to the body. One fell swoop. Now cut the leg at the second joint close to the body, cutting all the way down towards the "Pope's nose," that knob at the tail end, and trying to keep the crisp skin intact. Remove this section in one piece. (You can cut it into thigh and drumsticks sections after, if you please.) Do likewise to the other side.

3. With appendages removed, it's time to carve the white meat. Fork in breast, slice against the grain in neat, even pieces. Think deli slices. Or you can remove the breasts in two whole pieces if it's a chicken.

4. Presentation is key, so even if you butchered the bird, it's nothing some sprigs of parsley on a lovely platter can't fix.

ALMOND TART:
For to Look Like zee French Baker

—

Serves 12

Dough:

1 cup	all-purpose flour
1 tbsp	sugar
Pinch	salt
1/2 cup	cold unsalted butter, cut in small chunks
1/2 tsp	vanilla

Filling:

3/4 cup	whipping cream
1/2 cup	sugar
1 cup	sliced almonds
1 tbsp	dark rum
	Strawberries, for garnish (optional)

I learned how to make a version of this toothsome tart when I attended Le Cordon Bleu. In the French tradition we made our own puff pastry, used scales to measure ingredients (the European way) and wore starched whites and caps. This version allows for a simple dough, easy measuring and the wearing of jeans and sweatshirts. For it is the Canadian way.

1. To make the dough, mix flour with sugar and salt, then cut in cold butter until dough is blended into a fine meal. Add vanilla and work dough (with wooden spoon or cool hands) into a ball. Work quickly so dough doesn't heat up and melt butter. Press into a greased 9-inch tart pan with removeable bottom and freeze until hard, about 30 minutes.

2. Preheat oven to 425°F.

3. In a saucepan over medium heat, stir together cream and sugar. Simmer for 10 minutes, or until slightly thickened. Stir in almonds and rum. Set aside to cool for 10 minutes.

4. Place tart pan on a cookie sheet to catch possible spills and pour filling into tart shell. Bake for 25 to 30 minutes or until filling is bubbly and caramelized and the whole damn place smells like butter.

TO SERVE:

Let tart cool to room temperature, then put in fridge for an hour to help it set. Remove from pan. Slice into thin wedges and serve. For a nice garnish, slice some juicy strawberries up to the stems about five times, then fan out the cuts. One per customer.

SALTED VERSUS UNSALTED

Always use unsalted butter when baking: It's got that great creamery taste that gets passed on to your wholesome baked goods. Unsalted also lets you control the sodium content in your pastries. The one downside is that it doesn't keep as well as its salted counterpart (which keeps up to six months in the fridge owing to its salt-preservedness), so buy your unsalted butter in sticks, keep it in the freezer and defrost as needed. It's what the pros use.

QUÉBÉCOIS TARTE TATIN:
Je Me Souviens le Apple Pie

—

Serves 8–10

1/3 cup	unsalted butter
1/4 cup	sugar
6–8	Golden Delicious apples,* peeled, cored and quartered
1/4 cup	real maple syrup
1	block puff pastry (about 7 oz), thawed

*Don't substitute another variety. These apples have a low moisture content and hold their shape when cooked, which is key. Otherwise you might end up with Tarte au Applesauce. *Zut alors!*

Basically, you're going to roll out some store-bought dough, peel and slice apples, add butter and sugar and syrup and pop it in the oven. When it emerges all gloriously patisserie-like, you're going to have two choices: You can tell your friends it was easy. Or you can tell them it was hard. I'm not going to tell you how to run your life.

1. Butter a heavy, ovenproof frying pan (cast iron is best), then equally distribute the rest of the butter in small globs around the pan. Sprinkle sugar over butter. This will eventually make caramel.

2. Fit apple quarters snugly together in an overlapping circular formation, working your way into the centre with a spiral. Squeeze them in there. Pour maple syrup over apples.

3. Roll out puff pastry on a floured surface into a round about 1/4 inch thick. Lay over apples, tucking in around outer edge, and trim excess. Prick dough about 30 times with a fork.

4. Preheat oven to 450°F.

5. Place pan over medium-high heat until juices start to boil. Let apples cook until there is almost no liquid left in the pan and you begin to smell caramel, about 20 minutes.

6. Transfer pan to oven and bake until pastry is brown, about 10 minutes. Remove from oven

and jaggedly turn the pan, which releases the apples from the bottom and moves the caramel around. (Be as forceful as you are when trying to fit carry-on luggage into the overhead compartment.) Slide a small knife around the edge, making sure nothing is sticking. Cool on a rack.

TO SERVE:

Right before the ooh-la-la moment of turning out the tarte tatin, heat the pan over high heat for about 30 seconds, jiggling it to make sure nothing is sticking. Place a large serving plate over the pan, take a deep breath and flip the tarte onto the plate. Voilà! Sprinkle with icing sugar or side with vanilla ice cream.

VALUE ADDED BONUS
What to Do with the Other Half?

Stupid recipe calls for only half the package of pastry. What to do? Make another flaky French concoction, a pissaladière. Preheat oven to 450°F. Roll out pastry into a rectangle of cookie sheet size, throw onto a cookie sheet and prick dough with fork about 40 times. Place in fridge. In a frying pan melt 1 tbsp butter with 1 tbsp olive oil. Add two large onions, thinly sliced, along with a pinch of sugar, a pinch of salt and a splash of balsamic vinegar. Cook, stirring often, until caramelized, about twenty minutes. Smooth onion mixture over chilled pastry and bake for about twenty minutes, sprinkling with a crumbling of blue cheese in the last couple of minutes. Good hot or room temperature and makes for a great appetizer, or light lunch when sided with a fresh green salad.

DIM THE LIGHTS AND TURN UP THE HEAT:
Romantic repasts

The culinary arts may be new to you, but even the novice chef can knock the socks off her guy with a thoughtful menu plan, flattering candlelight and a leopard-print G-string. We all know that there are two ways to a man's heart, so why not hit him with this double-whammy and reap the rewards?

HAMACHI TARTARE:
When You Have Other Fish to Fry

Serves 2–4

4 oz	sushi-grade yellowtail (or tuna or salmon), finely chopped
1 tbsp	minced chives
1 tbsp	light soy sauce
1 tsp	minced fresh ginger
1 tsp	wasabi paste
1 tsp	olive oil
1/2 tsp	sesame oil
1 tbsp	vegetable oil
2	shallots, sliced
1 tbsp	toasted pine nuts
1/2	regular-size bag thick kettle-cooked potato chips (eat other half while cooking)

Hamachi is yellowtail fish, which is nice and light and fresh tasting, although you could do this with sushi-grade tuna or salmon as well. Did you notice how I said sushi-grade just then? You've got to tell your fishmonger what you're using his yellowtail for, and make sure it's impeccably fresh and clean and doesn't smell too fishy. Because if you serve your dude stinky tartare, you may soon be looking for another fish in the sea.

1. In a bowl combine yellowtail, chives, soy sauce, ginger, wasabi, olive oil and sesame oil.
2. In a small frying pan, heat vegetable oil over medium-high heat and cook shallots, stirring often, until deep brown and crunchy, about 7 to 10 minutes. Drain on paper towel.
3. Toss shallots and pine nuts in with tartare mixture.

TO SERVE:

Place a mound of your gorgeous tartare on two plates and side with a handful of potato chips, which you'll use as a vehicle for the fish. Or you can spoon some tartare on top of chips just before serving. Your call.

HOW TO FLIRT WITH YOUR FISHMONGER

He's got the high-grade seafood and fish you desire, and he could become one of the most important relationships you'll ever have. It's time to flirt like you've never flirted before.

1) Stare longingly at his hairnet and/or fishgut-soaked apron.
2) Gently stroke his mahi mahi.
3) Get a little crab tattooed on the back of your neck—tell him you did it for him. (He doesn't need to know you're a Cancer.)
4) Learn his name and be nice.

TOM YUM SOUP:
Thai Kickboxing in a Bowl

The first time I tasted this soup it was a revelation—flavour combinations I never could have imagined in my wildest dreams. Soothing and sour, earthy and fragrant. I booked my ticket to Thailand a week later. I stayed on for three months.

3 cups	fish stock
5	garlic cloves, whacked with the side of a knife
6	shallots, sliced
1	piece (2 inches) fresh ginger, peeled and sliced
2	stalks lemongrass, lower third only, cut in 1/2-inch slices
1/2 cup	sliced button mushrooms
3	large red chilies, cut in half lengthwise and seeded
3 tbsp	fish sauce
10 oz	fresh shrimp, peeled and deveined, tails left on
3 tbsp	lime juice
	Chopped fresh coriander, for garnish (optional)

1. In a large soup pot, bring stock to a boil. Add garlic, shallots, ginger and lemongrass. Keep boiling for a few minutes. Add mushrooms, chilies and fish sauce. Keep 'er boiling for 2 minutes more, then reduce to a simmer for 3 minutes. Add shrimp and simmer for 1 to 2 minutes or until they turn pink and become slightly firm. Remove from heat and stir in lime juice. Taste for seasoning and doctor it if need be. Trust your instincts.

TO SERVE:

Spoon it out, garnish with coriander and get ready for the ride of your life.

SURF-AND-TURF WITH PORT BUTTER:
Where Land and Sea Meet No-brainer

Serves 2

Port Butter:

3	shallots
1/2	small carrot, chopped
1/2 cup	port
1/4 cup	unsalted butter, at room temperature
	Salt and pepper to taste
1 lb	frozen snow crab legs, thawed
1	piece beef tenderloin (10 oz), cut in two medallions, at room temperature
1 tsp	olive oil
1/2 tsp	kosher salt
	A few cracks of pepper
1	bunch parsley, stems removed and leaves chopped
	Squirt of lemon
	Drizzle of olive oil
	Lemon wedges, for garnish

Splurge alert! When you want to go whole hog, this is a sensational and simple dish with a vino butter sauce and green-thumb side. It's like dating the high-school jock, homecoming queen and chess-club president all in one.

1. To make the port butter, mince 1 shallot and set aside. Chop remaining 2 shallots. In a small saucepan, combine chopped shallots, carrot and port. Reduce over medium-high heat to an almost syrupy consistency, then spoon out and discard veg or strain sauce through a sieve. There should be less than a tablespoon of liquid. Let cool in a bowl, then work in cubes of butter with a wooden spoon. It will look like there's no way it's going to come together, but it will. Stir in minced shallot and season with salt and pepper. Drain out any excess liquid by pressing butter mixture against side of bowl. Spoon butter in a line (about 6 inches) along a sheet of plastic wrap, then roll it up and twist the ends until it looks like a tubular hard candy. Put in fridge.

2. Boil or steam crab legs for about 4 minutes to heat through. Remove from pot and set aside.

3. If you're able to multi-task, heat a grill pan over high heat. Rub tenderloin medallions with oil and season with salt and pepper. Sear on all

sides and cook until medium-rare, 8 to 10 minutes. Let rest on a cutting board for 5 minutes.

4. Instead of the usual steakhouse parsley garnish, let's make the herb into a useful little salad. Toss parsley with a bit of lemon juice, olive oil and few grindings of salt and pepper.

TO SERVE:

Put a few warm crab legs on each plate along with a nice slab of tenderloin. Top turf with a slice of port butter and spruce up the dish with your parsley salad. Lemon wedges add extra panache, especially when squirted on crab legs. A bowl for discarded shells is a must. Fashioning the discarded exoskeletons into a glitter-painted parting gift is optional.

THE BEST BREAK-UPS INVOLVE A LITTLE PLANNING

When you're getting ready to spring the bad news on your soon-to-be ex, why not take the edge off with some soothing home-cooked favourites? Just as he's biting into his tenderloin and entering a comforting womb-like state, lay the news on him. Chances are he won't hate you and you can still be "friends." At worst, he hits the road fuming and you've got some yummy leftovers for Day 1 of your singledom.

SEARED SALADE NIÇOISE:
When You're This Good, You've Earned the Right to Be Arrogant
—

Serves 2

2	medium red potatoes, cut in half
2	large eggs, at room temperature
12	green beans (approx), ends tipped, cut in half crosswise
	Sea salt and cracked pepper
2	pieces fresh tuna steak (each 4 oz), at room temperature
1 tsp	sesame oil
1 tbsp	red wine vinegar
1/2 tsp	Dijon mustard
1	garlic clove, minced
Dash	Worcestershire sauce
3 tbsp	olive oil
1/2	small head romaine, washed and dried
	Handful of cherry tomatoes, washed and dried
	Handful of black olives (niçoise would be most appropriate)
1 tbsp	snipped chives

A French composition salad that may not be as easy as tossing together some airy field greens but isn't nearly as difficult as flying to Paris. With the modern twist of seared fresh tuna, it's truly a dish that belongs in the Louvre. Sorry, Charlie.

1. Put potatoes in a pot of cold water, bring to a boil and cook for 10 minutes. Add eggs and boil 6 minutes more. Drop in the green beans and boil for 4 minutes. Drain everything in a large colander. Remove potatoes and rinse beans and eggs under cold water. Cut potatoes into bite-sized chunks. Sprinkle with salt. Peel eggs and cut in half.

2. Heat a grill pan or nonstick frying pan over high heat. Coat tuna with sesame oil and sprinkle with salt and pepper. Sear tuna for 2 minutes on one side and 1 minute on the other. Remove from pan and set aside.

3. In a small bowl, whisk together vinegar, mustard, garlic and Worcestershire. While whisking, slowly drizzle in olive oil and whisk until combined. Add salt and pepper to taste.

TO SERVE:

Line two salad plates with bite-sized pieces of lettuce, arrange potatoes in the middle, and add beans, tomatoes and olives to your composition. Thinly slice seared tuna against the grain and lay slices over salad. Drizzle dressing over all, then add two half eggs to each plate. Sprinkle with a flourish of snipped chives. *La voilà!*

CHICKEN TAGINE:
From the Land of Snakecharmers and Storytellers

—

Serves 2

2	bone-in chicken breasts
	Sea salt and pepper
1 tbsp	harissa (recipe p.143)
1 tbsp	olive oil
1	small onion, sliced
1	garlic clove, minced
	Juice of 1 lemon
1/4 cup	water or chicken stock
1 tsp	lemon zest
1/4 cup	dried apricots, chopped
1/4 cup	black olives
1 cup	drained and rinsed canned chickpeas
1 tbsp	chopped fresh parsley
1 tbsp	chopped fresh coriander
1 tbsp	toasted slivered almonds (optional but good)

A clay tagine is the earthenware pot Moroccans use to prepare this delicious everyday dish. I got one for $3 in Marrakech, but you probably didn't, so here's a good way to relive the electric Djemaa el Fna square, without the subtle distractions of having a monkey thrown on your head for a $10 photo op.

1. Season chicken with salt and pepper, then coat with harissa. Marinate, covered and refrigerated, for 30 minutes.
2. In a large frying pan, heat oil over medium-high heat. Cook chicken until browned on both sides, about 5 minutes. Remove from pan and lower heat to medium.
3. Add onion and garlic and sauté until soft, a couple of minutes, adding a bit more oil if necessary. Add lemon juice and water and bring to a boil, stirring and scraping yummy bits off the bottom of the pan. Reduce heat to medium-low, return chicken to pan and stir in lemon zest, apricots, olives and chickpeas. Cover and cook for 15 to 20 minutes or until chicken is cooked through. Stir in herbs in the last minute. Sprinkle with toasted almonds.

TO SERVE:

If you can present this in a tagine, then you're my new favourite person. If not, I still like you, just not as much. The side dish of choice here would be couscous or cracked bulgur wheat that's ready to eat in 5 minutes.

SCARIEST NATIONAL DISH

If you ever find yourself in Marrakech's Djemaa el Fna square, you should work up the nerve to partake of Morocco's special-occasion dish, bastila (pronounced bas-teeya). The name comes from the Spanish word for pastry, *pastilla*, but after translation, the "p" turns into a "b" that is specific to the Arabic language. If, like me, you consider pigeons to be rats with wings, this will be the most challenging meal of your trip. These personal-sized pies are encased in a very thin phyllo-like pastry called *warqa* (which means leaf). They're filled with a healthy portion of chopped cooked pigeon and almonds, pan-fried and topped with a dusting of cinnamon and icing sugar. The sugar and fowl thing seems an odd mix, but so is the culinary history of contemporary Moroccan cuisine. It's basically an Arab and Hispano-Muslim diet based on an older and simpler Berber sustenance diet, with some sub-Saharan West African and colonial-era French influences thrown into the mix. Rating on the scary foods scale: a solid 9 out of 10, owing to the rats with wings thing.

2	large yams, cut in large wedges, wedges cut in half crosswise
1/4 cup	fresh or frozen cranberries
1/4 cup	real maple syrup
2 tbsp	unsalted butter, melted
	Salt and pepper to taste

MAPLE-GLAZED YAMS WITH CRANBERRIES:
For Bright Eyes and Bushy Tails

——

Serves 4

Tasty, pretty and easy. Remind you of anyone?

1. Preheat oven to 400°F.
2. Drop yams into an ovenproof pan, then toss with cranberries, syrup, melted butter, salt and pepper. Pop into the oven and bake for 40 minutes or until soft on inside, stirring halfway through.

TO SERVE:

Get 'em while they're hot; a great side dish to poultry. What's with the word "poultry," anyway? I hate it. Is it just me?

STEAK TARTARE:
Raw Is Sexy

—

Serves 2

It may seem barbaric, but there's nothing like eating death-defying raw meat to put you in the mood for *l'amour*. After all, this could be your last night on Earth. Thought to be aphrodisiacs, raw foods are sensual in look, taste and feel. Best of all, you don't have to sweat over a hot stove cooking them, so you can save the sweating for later on, when you're cookin' in the sack.

Go to a good butcher for the freshest, best beef. Tell him what it's for. He'll set you up, and maybe even pass it through the grinder once.

8 oz	ground best-quality tenderloin
1 tbsp	extra virgin olive oil
	Sea salt and cracked pepper to taste
1 tsp	Worcestershire sauce
1 tsp	Dijon mustard
2	intact egg yolks (shells washed and reserved)
2	small shallots, minced
1 tbsp	minced capers (drained and rinsed first)
4	gherkins, minced
2 tbsp	minced fresh parsley

1. In a bowl, mix impeccably fresh chopped beef with oil, salt, pepper, Worcestershire and mustard. Form meat into two patties.

HEALTH ALERT:
This dish is not to be consumed by the frail, elderly, wee tots, people with heart murmurs or vegetarians.

TO SERVE:

Get out two plates and place a patty, off centre, on each plate. Press an indentation into each patty and place a washed half eggshell in each. Gently drop an egg yolk in each shell. Arrange the other ingredients in mini mounds around the beef. Take a forkful of meat. Dip in egg yolk and then in other accoutrements. Godspeed.

MILK CHOCOLATE SAUCE:
The Lickable Body Mask

1/2 cup	whipping cream
6 oz	good-quality milk chocolate, broken in chunks

Makes about 1 cup

Poured over ice cream, drizzled on sponge cake, painted across body parts: is there nothing this sauce can't do? Backrubs cost. You can add your favourite liqueur to further spruce things up. Simply add a tablespoon of spirits to the cream before heating and proceed as usual.

1. Heat whipping cream to the point just before it boils. Remove from heat and stir in chocolate until smooth. Let cool. Ta-da!

TO SERVE:
Drizzle it on warm and thick. Don't be shy.

COOKING TIP
The sauce will firm up in the fridge. To get it runny again, pop it in the micro for 10 seconds and stir.

A potent cocktail gives the illusion of looking flushed with love, even if the feelings aren't quite there yet. Not to worry, the night is young.

MARGARITAS
Rub the rims of two chilled cocktail glasses with lime slice and dip the moist rims in salt. To a martini shaker two-thirds full of ice, add tequila, Triple Sec and lime juice. Shake like you've never shaken before. Strain into prepared glasses.

1	slice of lime
Pinch	kosher salt
3 oz	tequila
2 oz	Triple Sec
	Juice of 1 small lime

A BOTTLE OF YOUR FINEST
Champagne gets the job done every time. It's what we call "a closer" in the biz. Serve in champagne glasses or flutes—or straight from your stilettos. This will make for a night of all kinds of cork popping.

ME TOO

I FANCY A G&T

JUICY GIN
To a martini shaker two-thirds full of ice, add gin and juices. Shake hard. Strain into two chilled highball glasses with a few ice cubes in each, and top with tonic water. A citrus twist on my favourite drink.

4 oz	gin
	Juice of 1/2 lemon
	Juice of 1/2 orange
	Tonic water

CHAMPAGNE AND STILETTOS:
Cocktail party sips and nibbles

It's time to show off your inner fabulousness while becoming the envy of your friends and networking your way to six figures. Get ready to throw the party of your life. Pop the invitations in the mail, write a detailed to-do list, buy more booze than necessary (splurge on your friends) and prepare a cornucopia of delectable bites (even though anyone who brings a discriminating palate to a party is probably someone you don't want there).

Here are some basic etiquette tips for keeping your soiree smooth sailing. A) One should never expect hostess gifts from guests, but if they do arrive empty-handed feel free to announce this to the party: "Hey, everyone, Jim and Sally are here and they didn't bring me a damn thing!" Wine, chocolates and flowers are always useful and appreciated in a party scenario. B) Nobody derives joy from a stressed-out hostess. Loosen up and relax. Hint: Do a few body shots before your revellers arrive. C) Display impeccable manners and your guests will follow suit. This may be the party that finally transcends your usual drunken keggers!

EGGPLANT CAVIAR WITH HOMEMADE PITA CRISPS:
The Recession-busting Snack

Serves 4

Eggplant Caviar:

1	large eggplant (about 18 oz)
1/4 cup	extra virgin olive oil
2 tbsp	fresh lemon juice
1	garlic clove, minced
1/2 tsp	salt
1/4 tsp	freshly ground black pepper
1 tbsp	chopped capers (drained and rinsed first)
2 tbsp	chopped fresh parsley
1 tbsp	chopped fresh basil leaves
Pinch	sugar

Pita Crisps:

4	Greek-style pitas
1 tbsp	olive oil
	Paprika, garlic powder
	Salt and pepper to taste

Love it or loathe it, caviar does make a statement. Present a pricey little iced canister to your guests and no matter what other crap you serve, they'll retell the tale of how your party was the utmost in decadence: "Caviar even!" This easy appetizer deliciously thumbs its nose at food snobs.

1. Preheat oven to 400°F.
2. Place eggplant on a baking sheet and pierce several times with a fork. Bake until soft and skin is cracked and wrinkled, about 45 minutes. Let cool to the point that you can touch it without crying out in pain, then cut in half lengthwise. Peel off skin, place skinned eggplant in colander and let drain 45 minutes. Finely chop eggplant.
3. Whisk together olive oil, lemon juice and garlic in a medium bowl. Season with salt and pepper. Stir in eggplant, then toss in capers, parsley, basil and a pinch of sugar if eggplant tastes slightly bitter. Cover and refrigerate for at least an hour.
4. Brush each pita with olive oil. Sprinkle with paprika, garlic powder, salt and pepper, then cut each pita into eight wedges. Spread out evenly on baking sheet and bake for 7 to 10 minutes or until browned.

TO SERVE:

Dress in sensible flats, an oversized, florally hat and a crimson feather boa. Pour the eggplant caviar into a prized serving piece and encircle the bowl with warm pita crisps. Then walk around the room doing your best Mrs. Howell: "Caviar, darling?"

WHAT TO DO WITH BAD HOSTESS GIFTS

When did awful, flavoured vinegars and obnoxious spice mixes become the hostess gifts du jour? If I want a loaf tin, a dishtowel—and your "famous" banana nut bread recipe, I'll ask for it, thanks. Then again, sometimes reject gifts can be turned around in a few easy steps:

1. **THE GIFT:** Olive oil in fancy bottle.
   THE SOLUTION: Decant oil and refill ornate bottle with brandy. Keep on work desk for "emergencies."

2. **THE GIFT:** Yet another "15 hour" eucalyptus candle.
   THE SOLUTION: Keep on desk and use to warm brandy.

3. **THE GIFT:** Stupid cellophane-wrapped mug filled with stale jellybeans.
   THE SOLUTION: Throw candy at gift-giver while using mug to enjoy brandy.

TRIO OF OLIVE, GORGONZOLA AND WILD MUSHROOM CROSTINI:
A Roman Toast

—

Serves 8–10

1/2 cup	finely chopped, pitted Kalamata olives
1 tsp	olive oil
3 tbsp	finely chopped fresh parsley
2	garlic cloves, minced
1/2 tsp	black pepper
5 oz	Gorgonzola cheese, crumbled
2 tbsp	unsalted butter, softened
1/8 tsp	cayenne
1/2 lb	fresh mushrooms, chopped (white button will do, but earthy wild ones are a tad more adventurous)
1/4 tsp	salt
1 tbsp	dry vermouth
2	baguettes, cut in 1/2-inch slices on a slight angle
	A handful of pitted Kalamata olives, for garnish (optional)
	A handful of toasted whole almonds, for garnish (optional)
	Parsley sprigs, for garnish (optional)

Crostini are delicious toasts with a difference. Topped with olive tapenade, wild mushroom ragout or Gorgonzola spread, every bite takes you back to Italy and a moveable Roman feast.

1. In a small bowl, combine olives, olive oil, 1 tbsp of the parsley, half the garlic, and 1/4 tsp black pepper. Beat into a pulpy mixture. Set aside.

2. In another small bowl, combine Gorgonzola cheese, 1 tbsp of the butter, cayenne and 1 tbsp of the parsley. Stir until combined. Set aside.

3. In a medium frying pan, melt remaining 1 tbsp butter on medium-high heat. Add garlic and stir for 30 seconds. Add chopped mushrooms and salt; cook, stirring frequently, until most of the liquid has evaporated, about 5 minutes. Add the vermouth and cook for another minute. Remove from heat and stir in remaining 1 tbsp parsley.

4. Preheat broiler. Place baguette slices on a cookie sheet and broil until lightly toasted. Flip them over and do likewise on the other side. Repeat until all of the bread (now we can call them crostini) is toasted.

TO SERVE:

Spread each crostini with one of your prepared toppings (olive tapenade, Gorgonzola spread or wild mushroom ragout, if inquisitive guests ask). Top the olive ones with an olive, the Gorgonzola ones with an almond and the mushroom ones with a parsley sprig so they don't feel left out.

PREPPING YOURSELF FOR THE PARTY

1. Mix yourself a big old cocktail.
2. Exfoliate.
3. Repeat the mantra "I'm the hostess with the mostess."
4. Rehydrate often.

SAVOURY DIPPERS WITH SPICY MUSTARD SAUCE:
Great Balls of Spinach

Serves 8–10

Spicy Mustard Sauce:

1/2 cup	mustard powder
1/2 cup	white vinegar
1/4 cup	sugar
1	egg yolk

Spinach Balls:

2	pkg (10 oz each) frozen spinach, thawed
2 cups	herbed stuffing mix,* crushed (e.g., 1 box of Pepperidge Farm or Stove Top)
1 cup	grated Parmesan cheese
1/2 cup	unsalted butter, melted
4	green onions, finely chopped
3	eggs, beaten
2 tbsp	chopped fresh parsley, for garnish

*Some stuffing mixes come with two bags in the box, the stuffing mixture plus a seasoning packet. Crush the stuffing, then stir in the seasoning.

These easy, mouth-watering bites aren't just tasty, they're useful too. It's unlikely there will be any left-over balls, but if there are a stray few, why not glue on some backings and make them into yummy and chic earrings? (Don't forget to save some mustard dip in the glove compartment.) Or paint faces onto your spinach balls and use them as action figures for hours of fun! Popeye would be proud.

Make the mustard sauce a day ahead if you can. It's stunningly delicious and worth the wait. (In a pinch, a jar of honey mustard does just fine as a sub for the sauce.)

1. First we'll make the mustard sauce, because it should be prepared about 5 hours in advance of serving. If you plan to serve the balls with store-bought honey mustard, skip ahead to step 2. For the rest of you, all you do to make the sauce is combine the mustard powder and vinegar in a small bowl and let it stand for 4 hours. When the time is up, blend the sugar and egg yolk in a small saucepan and stir in the mustard mixture. Cook over low heat, stirring constantly, until it thickens slightly, about 10 minutes. Cover and chill for at least half an hour.

2. Preheat oven to 350°F. Spray a cookie sheet with nonstick cooking spray.

3. Using your hands and all of your strength, squeeze the water out of the spinach until it's as dry as you can get it. Mix the spinach with the stuffing mix, Parmesan, butter, green onions and eggs with your hands until combined. Form into 1-inch balls and arrange on cookie sheet. Bake for 10 to 15 minutes or until firm. (Balls can be made a day ahead and warmed up in a 200°F oven before serving. Also tasty at room temperature.)

TO SERVE:

Pour the cold mustard sauce into a pretty little dish and set it in the centre of a large plate. Pile the spinach balls up and around (but not in) the sauce bowl, and garnish with a sprinkle of parsley.

PARTY HYGIENE

It may be called a toothpick, but the last time anyone actually used it as such, Paul Lynde was sitting centre square. Do not use a toothpick in public for the purposes of teeth cleaning. Yes, the handy wooden skewer sticking out of the Swedish meatball (now so painfully lodged beside your left incisor) is seemingly the perfect implement for unwedging that errant piece of meat, but using a toothpick for matters of dental hygiene is the height of poor manners. And while we're discussing, using a strand of hair as makeshift dental floss is never acceptable.

HE WANTED TO BE A TOOTHPICK.

I HATE THIS JOB

MUSHROOM CIGARS:
Monica's Favourite

—

Makes about 36 pieces

3 tbsp plus 1/4 cup	unsalted butter
1/2 lb	fresh mushrooms, minced (I wouldn't say no to a hand blender)
2	medium shallots, finely chopped
1/2 tsp	salt
1/4 tsp	black pepper
1 tbsp	Madeira or sweet sherry (or lemon juice if need be)
1 tsp	red wine or balsamic vinegar
1/4 cup	sour cream
6	sheets phyllo dough, thawed and kept in wax paper under a damp tea towel

This is the perfect party dish to prepare when you want to impress people without really doing the work. Kind of like cheating on a math test. Or with a president.

1. In a large frying pan, melt 3 tbsp of the butter over medium-high heat. Add mushrooms and shallots, season with salt and pepper, and cook, stirring frequently, for several minutes. Stir in Madeira and vinegar. Keep cooking slowly, stirring often, until almost all of the liquid has evaporated from the mixture, 7 to 10 minutes; it will be a little bit stiff but still mushy. Let cool slightly, then stir in sour cream. Taste for seasoning.
2. Preheat oven to 375°F.
3. Melt remaining 1/4 cup butter. Carefully cut a sheet of phyllo into six rectangles, approximately 4 1/2 by 7 inches. Lightly brush each one with some melted butter. Spread 1 teaspoon mushroom mixture along a short end of each rectangle, leaving a 1/2-inch border. Fold the long edges over slightly and roll up into a little cigar.
4. Grease a cookie sheet with melted butter and place your cigars, seam side down, on the sheet. Lightly brush cigars with melted butter. Repeat with the rest of the mushroom mixture and phyllo sheets. Bake for 10 to 15 minutes or until golden brown.

TO SERVE:

Can be served hot or at room temperature. To keep warm, leave in a 200°F oven until your guests arrive.

PARTY STAIN REMOVAL TIPS
FOR DRINKS AND/OR BODILY FLUIDS

If your fabrics are washable (read: not dry clean only), for best results try to treat stains within 24 hours. Older stains are more difficult to remove (right, Monica?). For tannin stains, which would include the likes of beer, wine, citrus juices and soft drinks, toss offending garments in the washer with detergent and warm or hot water. If trace stains remain, soak in an all-fabric bleach solution for 5 minutes. Don't rub the stain with soap if you don't have time to do laundry, because soap sets tannin stains, so you really wouldn't be helping matters, would you?

I FEEL LIKE A SUBSTITUTE FOR ANOTHER GUY..

MINI SWEET POTATO LATKES:
Frilly Little Orange Numbers

—

Serves 10–15

4	medium sweet potatoes, peeled and grated
1	small onion, grated
1	garlic clove, minced
2	eggs, beaten
1/4 cup	minced fresh parsley
1/2 tsp	salt
1/4 tsp	cracked pepper
3/4 cup	all-purpose flour
1/2 cup	vegetable oil

PARTY TIP
Make a bit ahead of time and keep warm on cookie sheets in a 200°F oven.

This is a twist on the favourite Chanukah mainstay, for the modern Jewish American Princess.

1. Once you've grated and minced everything, the hard part is over. I'm sorry I had to do that to you. But it's over now and I think you're a better person for it. Now just mix together the sweet potatoes, onion, garlic, eggs, parsley, salt and pepper. Then stir in the flour.

2. In a large frying pan over medium-high heat, heat 2 tbsp of the oil. Drop in the batter 1 tbsp at a time, flattening the pancakes out a bit. Cook for several minutes on each side until golden brown and crispy. Remove latkes as they cook and set aside on a dish lined with paper towel. Add more oil to the pan as needed, and keep cooking till your batter is gone.

TO SERVE:
Make the mango chutney (p. 143) for a seductive mix of sweet and salty, soft and crunchy. Pass 'em around while they're good and hot.

SPICED MIXED OLIVES:
Ban the Martini! Free the Olive!

___

Serves a crowd

Is it just me, or are olives the bits 'n' bites of the '00s?

1. Toss all ingredients together in a bowl and let sit at room temperature for a few hours.

TO SERVE:
Pour into a decorative bowl, with a side bowl for pits. Rustic-chic.

4 cups	mixed good-quality olives, green ones, black ones, large and small, rinsed (available at most supermarket delis)
2	garlic cloves, thinly sliced
1	small lemon, cut into wedges and roughly chopped
2 tsp	chopped fresh rosemary, or 1 tsp crumbled dried
2 tsp	chili flakes
1/2 tsp	pepper
1/4 cup	extra virgin olive oil

ENTERTAINING TIP
If someone useful offers to help you prepare your shindig, SAY YES.

BAKED BRIE:
Cheese Wheel Keeps on Turning, Proud Mary Keeps on Eating

—

Serves 8–10

1/4 cup	dried cranberries
1/2 cup	chopped pecans, toasted
1/4 cup	brown sugar
1 tsp	orange zest
4	sheets phyllo dough, thawed and kept in wax paper under a damp tea towel
1/2 cup	unsalted butter, melted
1	wheel (1 lb) brie
	Melba or Paris toasts or your favourite plain crackers

Why is it that we never eat brie unless it's on some sweaty cheese tray at a Christmas cocktail party? It's ridiculous, and I hereby pledge to change that. One wheel at a time.

1. In a small bowl, stir together cranberries, pecans, sugar and orange zest.

2. Working with one sheet of phyllo at a time (keep remaining dough under damp towel), brush with melted butter. Lay a second sheet of dough over the first, then brush it with butter. Place brie in centre of dough, spread cranberry mixture on top and pat down firmly. Fold edges of phyllo up to the centre of the cheese. Brush another sheet of dough with butter, lay the last sheet on top and brush it with butter. Place wrapped brie, folded edges down, in the centre of prepared sheets, then fold up edges of dough. Brie should be fully encased with no chance of escape. Brush entire round with butter. Place brie on a cookie sheet and refrigerate for at least 30 minutes.

3. Preheat oven to 425°F.

4. Bake brie for 15 to 20 minutes or until golden. Allow to rest for 15 minutes before serving.

TO SERVE:

Bring it out on a tray with several knives for cutting and spreading the fondue-like ooze. And don't worry if you run out of crackers. People will just bend over and eat it with their faces.

PARTY TIP
Remove all chairs. It encourages mingling— and dancing.

HONEY-CURED GRAVLAX:
A Danish Delicacy with a Pooh Bear Twist

—

Serves a large party

1	whole skin-on side of boneless fresh salmon (2 1/2–3 lb)
2 lb	sugar (approx)
1 1/4 lb	kosher salt (approx)
2/3 cup	liquid honey
1	bunch fresh dill, reserve about 2 tbsp chopped sprigs for garnish
	Cocktail pumpernickel or moist rye bread squares
	Honey mustard

Although this elegant appetizer takes 48 hours to make, there's really only about 15 minutes of active prep time. That means while your salmon is self-curing, you're free to go to the spa or get back in touch with long-lost friends. Luckily, the fish is dead, so you're the only one left to reap the raves.

1. Mix sugar and salt together. Get out a tray large enough to hold the salmon and evenly spread half the sugar-salt mixture in the tray. Place side of salmon on sugar-salt mixture, skin side down. Evenly pour honey over fish.
2. Completely cover salmon with most of the remaining sugar-salt mixture, carefully packing it down so no pink is showing. (Reserve a bit of the mixture to seal broken spots, which can happen after about 12 hours.) Lay dill over sugar and salt (it will permeate), cover with plastic wrap and put in the fridge for 48 hours.
3. After a couple of days, the salmon is cured. Carefully wash off the sugar and salt with cool water and pat dry.

TO SERVE:
Peel or slice off skin. Starting at the tail end, cut salmon against the grain into thin slices. Serve on top of bread spread with a touch of honey mustard, and top with a sprig of dill. Um, are you a caterer or something?

GUACAMOLE QUESADILLAS:
El Loco Snacko

If pairing sweet red pepper with smooth avocado, tart lime juice and zippy Jack cheese is wrong, I don't want to be right.

1. In a medium bowl, stir together cream cheese, red pepper, lime juice, sugar, coriander, jalapeño, avocado and green onions.
2. Spread a heaping tablespoon of the cream cheese mixture on a tortilla. Top with an even sprinkling of shredded Monterey Jack cheese, then cover with another tortilla. Press down a bit so the two tortillas stick together, forming a quesadilla.
3. Preheat oven to 200°F.
4. In a large frying pan, heat 1 tsp oil over medium heat. Cook a quesadilla until golden on one side, then flip and do likewise on the other. Drain on paper towel, then place on a cookie sheet. Repeat until you have five gorgeous quesadillas. Keep warm on cookie sheets in the oven until your guests arrive.

TO SERVE:

Cut each quesadilla into four wedges and pile 'em high. A little salsa perfects this Mexican miracle.

4 oz	cream cheese, softened
1	red pepper, finely chopped
1 1/2 tbsp	fresh lime juice
Pinch	sugar
1 tbsp	minced fresh coriander
1	jalapeño pepper, seeded and minced
1	large avocado, chopped
2	green onions, chopped
10	8-inch flour tortillas
1 cup	shredded Monterey Jack cheese
2 tbsp	vegetable oil (approx)
	Salsa (optional)

IS *EVERYBODY* HAPPY?:
Pitcher Drinks for a Crowd
—

If you go through the trouble of throwing a party and decide not to mix up a signature cocktail, then you're really missing the point.

1/2	small seedless watermelon, frozen overnight
	Juice of 2 limes, juiced halves reserved
6 oz	tequila
2 tsp	sugar, plus extra to rim glasses

FROZEN WATERMELON MARGARITA
Serves 4–6

1. Cut frozen watermelon into chunks, discarding rind, and put watermelon, lime juice, tequila and sugar in a blender. Buzz until smooth. You might have to do this in two batches. Run the juiced lime halves around the rims of chilled serving glasses, then dip rims in a plate of sugar. Let dry for a minute, then pour and serve.

4 cups	red wine (preferably Spanish)
4 oz	brandy
4 oz	Cointreau or Triple Sec
	Juice of 1 lemon
1 tbsp	sugar
2	oranges, sliced
2	apples, cored and diced
2	limes, sliced
4 cups	club soda

A VAT OF SANGRIA
Serves about 8

1. This should be made a few hours in advance. Stir together wine, brandy, Cointreau, lemon juice and sugar until sugar dissolves, then add fruit. Put in fridge to chill. Before serving, add soda water and ice. Serve in chilled pitchers and pour into red wine glasses.

HOW TO MIX THE PERFECT COCKTAIL

Start with a classic recipe: There are several here, and many more are interspersed throughout this wonderful book. I got these tips from the bar manager at my favourite watering hole in Vancouver, a spot dedicated to the renaissance of cocktails from a time when men drank like men and women also drank like men. When mixing your cocktails, use only freshly squeezed citrus juices and good liquor and liqueurs, but not necessarily premium brands. Never add artificial flavours or colours. As for the mixing, shake each drink vigorously with fresh ice. A drink requires only about 10 seconds of shaking to be flash frozen, but you need to shake it *hard.* Free-pour your whisky, but measure your cocktails. And always offer up a toast before downing your beverage. Makes for good excuses for drinking that many more.

1/2	bottle (375 mL) Sauternes
1 1/4 cup	pineapple juice
	Juice of 1 lemon
2 tbsp	sugar
1	750 mL bottle chilled dry champagne (or high-quality sparkling wine)

CELEBRATORY CHAMPAGNE COOLIES
Serves 8–10

1. Stir together Sauternes, pineapple juice and sugar until sugar dissolves. Plop a couple of ice cubes into 8 to 10 highball glasses, divide cocktail mixture evenly, then top each glass with champagne. Celebrate good times, come on.

DRINKS HINT
The cardinal rule when it comes to cocktail parties (among my group of friends) is when the booze runs out, so do the guests. I should probably align myself with a better class of friends.

NO I'M NOT

The world is
our oyster

WHY CAN'T WE ALL JUST GET ALONG?:
Bridge-building international favourites

You're a woman of the world: a been-there, done-that globe-trotting gal, a continental cook who adores foreign flavours. Lift the heavenly scented veil of secrecy off recipes from far-away places. Introduce your homebody pals to the global village. Far-flung Thailand, the culinary magic carpet ride of Morocco and exotic India, to name a few. Hola, Spain! Ciao, Italy! Irie, Jamaica! Mexico—Cómo estás?

SZECHUAN CARROT SOUP:
You Got Your Carrot in My Peanut Butter!

—

Serves 4–6

1 tsp	vegetable oil
1	onion, chopped
2	garlic cloves, minced
6	large carrots, peeled and chopped
1	piece (1 inch) fresh ginger, peeled and minced
1/4 tsp	cayenne or chili flakes
4 cups	vegetable or chicken stock
2 tbsp	creamy peanut butter
4 tsp	soy sauce
1 tsp	sugar
	A few drops sesame oil

I know it seems like an odd mix, but you're just going to have to trust me on this one.

1. Heat vegetable oil in a large saucepan over medium heat. Add onion and garlic; cook, stirring frequently, for a couple of minutes until softened. Add carrots, ginger, cayenne and stock. Bring to a boil, reduce to a simmer, cover and cook for 30 minutes.
2. Remove from heat and add peanut butter, soy sauce, sugar and sesame oil. Using a hand blender, purée the soup in the pot. Reheat over low heat until it's hot enough to eat, without letting it boil.

TO SERVE:
Don't quote me on this . . . bowls and soupspoons?

MEXICAN LIME SOUP:
Viva la Soupa!

Serves 6

Imagine: eight 18-year-old university students let loose in Mexico for a week during spring break, with few inhibitions and a fistful of cash. Two firsts on that trip: drinking enough tequila to cause temporary blindness, and eating this tangy tortilla soup.

1. Juice 1 lime and thinly slice the other one.
2. In a large saucepan, melt butter over medium-high heat. Add shallots and sauté until softened, 3 to 4 minutes. Add tomato and jalapeño; cook for another 2 minutes. Stir in stock, lime juice and sugar. Cover and simmer for 20 minutes. Stir in chicken and tequila and heat through. Season with pepper.

TO SERVE:
Garnish with lime slices, a handful of tortilla chips, avocado and a sprinkling of coriander.

2	limes
1 tbsp	unsalted butter
4	small shallots, finely chopped
1	large tomato, peeled (see sidebar) and finely chopped
1	jalapeño pepper, seeded and minced
6 cups	chicken stock
Pinch	sugar
1 cup	shredded cooked chicken (buy a couple of pieces of BBQd chick at the supermarket deli)
1 tbsp	tequila
	Cracked pepper to taste
	Tortilla chips, for garnish
1	avocado, cubed, for garnish
1 tbsp	chopped fresh coriander, for garnish (optional)

HOW TO PEEL A TOMATO
Cut a shallow cross with the point of a knife on the bottom of the tomato, then plunge it into a small pot of boiling water for 30 seconds. Run the tomato under cold water. The skin should begin to lift at the cross, and from there you can grab and peel. Kind of like your skin after a bad sunburn.

INDIAN BUTTER CHICKEN WITH ALMOND RICE:
Better than Finding Inner Peace

Serves 4

3 tbsp	unsalted butter
1	medium onion, cut in 8 wedges
1/4 tsp	cinnamon
2	garlic cloves, minced
1 tbsp	minced fresh ginger
1 tsp	turmeric
1 tsp	chili powder
1/4 tsp	cayenne
1 lb	skinless, boneless chicken breasts, cut in bite-sized pieces
1/2 cup	ground almonds
1 cup	canned plum tomatoes with juice
1/2 cup	plain yogurt
1 tbsp	chopped fresh coriander
	Salt and pepper to taste

Rice:

2 cups	chicken stock, boiling
2 tbsp	unsalted butter
1 cup	unconverted rice (read: not the five-minute kind)
1	small onion, finely chopped
Pinch	salt
1/4 cup	slivered almonds, toasted
1 tbsp	minced fresh parsley (optional)

Yes, the ingredients list looks lengthy, but Indian food is all about the gentle balance of spices and seasonings. And achieving the divine end result takes a lengthy list of spices and seasonings. Once the chicken's in the pan, get going on the rice. One of the keys to successful cooking is timing. Comedy too.

1. In a large frying pan over medium heat, melt butter until it is frothy. Add onion and cinnamon and fry until onion is soft. Stir in garlic, ginger, turmeric, chili and cayenne. Stir around for a minute. Smelling like paradise.

2. Stir in chicken and cook until chicken has turned white. Add ground almonds and tomatoes with their juice. Mix it all up, cover and simmer for 20 to 25 minutes until chicken is cooked through.

3. While chicken is simmering, make the accompanying luscious rice. In a small saucepan or the microwave, bring chicken stock to a boil. In a medium saucepan, melt butter over medium heat. Stir in rice and onion. Cook, stirring constantly, for 2 minutes. Pour in hot chicken stock, add a goodly pinch of salt, give a big old stir, reduce heat to low, cover and simmer for 20 minutes.

4. When time is up and all the liquid has been absorbed, stir in toasted almonds and let sit,

covered, for 5 minutes. Then stir in parsley, if using.

5. Meanwhile, stir yogurt and coriander into chicken. Add salt and pepper, and heat through.

TO SERVE:

Look at you, you just made a delicious Indian feast! Serve up the chicken, side it with the rice, and if you're feeling extra generous, cook up some crunchy papadam. There's a quick way to make this favourite bread (see bonus recipe). It involves 40 extra seconds of your time.

I HATE BEING OPTIONAL — GO ON, EAT ME.

CAJUN JAMBALAYA:
In N'Awleans, Even Rice Is a Party

Serves 6

3 tbsp	vegetable oil
3	boneless, skinless chicken breasts, cubed
1/2 lb	spicy smoked sausage, sliced (Cajun-style is best)
2 tsp	brown sugar
2 cups	chopped onions
1 cup	chopped celery
1 cup	chopped red pepper
3	garlic cloves, minced
2 1/2 cups	chicken stock
1 tsp	paprika
1/2 tsp	cayenne
2 cups	long-grain rice
1/2 lb	fresh shrimp, peeled and deveined, tails left on
1/2 cup	chopped green onions
	Salt and pepper to taste

In Louisiana, this one-pot meal is known as rice with a gift.

1. In a large saucepan over medium-high heat, sauté chicken in 2 tbsp of the oil until lightly browned. Add sausage and stir about for a couple of minutes to meld flavours (smoked sausage is already cooked, so don't get your knickers in a knot). Remove meat from pot and set aside.

2. Reduce heat to medium and add remaining 1 tbsp oil. Stir in brown sugar; let the sugar melt and brown a bit. Add onions, celery, red pepper and garlic. Sauté for a couple of minutes until veggies wilt and onion becomes transparent. Pour in stock and stir around, scraping brown bits off bottom. Return chicken and sausage to the pot, stir in paprika and cayenne. Stir in rice. Bring to a boil.

3. Cover pot, reduce heat and simmer for 15 minutes. Give her a big stir from the bottom. Add shrimp and cook for another 7 to 10 minutes, or until rice is tender. Stir in green onions, salt and pepper.

TO SERVE:
Ooowee, that's some good jambalaya. Now eat her up while she be good and hot.

A SHORT FOOD HISTORY LESSON
Learning Is Good

New Orleans has always been a melting pot of ethnic diversity. Africans, Spaniards, Frenchmen, Choctaw Indians and especially the Acadians who came via Canada's eastern shores—all had a hand in the city's spicy style of cookin'. Creole is the traditional New Orleans cuisine, a word that refers to the descendants of the city's French and Spanish colonists, but it has evolved to include the European, Caribbean and African settlers. The Acadians', or "Cajuns'," ancestors settled the French colony of Acadie in eastern Canada during the seventeenth century, and resettled in Louisiana after being expelled from the territory when it came under British rule. They were the creators of Cajun food. Creole and Cajun dishes are as alike as they are different. They share a number of ingredients, including a thickener of roux (flour browned in oil or animal fat) for gumbos and jambalaya, both of which can be Creole or Cajun. The main difference between the two is that Cajun recipes are usually based on pork, poultry, fish or shellfish, whereas Creole dishes have a lot of those same ingredients but come with an additional European panache. The most obvious example is the use of cream or butter sauces, an influence brought over by French immigrants. Either way, it's all good, honeychild.

A TRIO OF SPICY SAUCES FROM FAR-OFF LANDS:
Hot Stuff Coming Through!
—

Here are some foreign condiments to help you relive fond travels to Exotica, or to simply aid in yumminess. Think global. Eat local.

CHILI JAM
Hint: turns a good cheese plate into a great one.
Makes about 3/4 cup

3	small shallots, thinly sliced
1/2 cup	sugar
1/2 cup	seeded and minced jalapeño peppers (about 3 medium)
1/4 cup	minced red pepper
1/4 cup	water
	Juice of 1/2 lime
1/4 tsp	salt

1. Combine all ingredients in a medium saucepan over high heat and bring to a boil. Reduce heat to medium, and keep it at a low boil, stirring often, until reduced by half, about 20 minutes. Let cool a bit, then pour into a bowl and refrigerate.

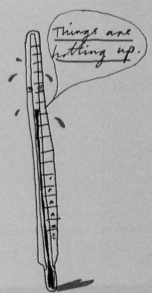

Things are hotting up.

3/4 cup	brown sugar
3/4 cup	vinegar
1 1/2 cups	diced mango
1	garlic clove, minced
1 tsp	minced fresh ginger
Dash	Tabasco sauce
Pinch	salt
1 tbsp	finely chopped fresh coriander
1/4 cup	toasted and chopped macadamia nuts (optional)

MANGO CHUTNEY

Hint: I cannot eat
Indian food without it.

Makes about 1 1/2 cups

1. Pour sugar and vinegar into a medium saucepan, place over medium heat, bring to a boil and cook, stirring occasionally, until the liquid reduces and thickens. Stir in mango, garlic, ginger, Tabasco and salt; simmer for 5 minutes. Remove from heat and stir in coriander. Let the mixture cool to room temperature, then refrigerate for a few hours. Stir in nuts, if using, and purée with a hand blender.

2 tbsp	cayenne
2 tbsp	ground cumin
1 tsp	sea salt
3 tbsp	fresh lemon juice
1 tsp	lemon zest
1/2 cup	olive oil
	Cracked pepper to taste

HARISSA

Hint: like ketchup to Moroccans.
See Chicken Tagine recipe on p.110.

Makes about 3/4 cup

1. Mix all ingredients together and store in the fridge. Bring to room temperature and give it a stir before using.

SWEET BROILED EGGPLANT:
Miso Horny

—

Serves 4

2	small Asian eggplants (small, purple, long and lean)
2 tsp	vegetable oil
1/4 cup	sweet miso paste (see p. 155)
2 tbsp	mirin (see p. 13)
1/4 cup	sake
	Cracked pepper

I envy the Japanese their exquisite traditions and good taste. I really do.

1. Preheat oven to 400°F. Line a cookie sheet with foil.
2. Cut the ends off of each eggplant, then cut eggplants in half lengthwise. Place cut sides up on the cookie sheet and rub with a little oil. Bake for 20 minutes or until cooked through and taking on a bit of colour. Remove from oven and turn on broiler.
3. In a small bowl, stir together miso paste, mirin, sake and pepper to taste. Slather mixture on top of each eggplant.
4. Back in the oven they go for a few minutes, until sauce is bubbling and browned.

TO SERVE:

It tastes exactly like what you'd get in a Japanese restaurant! You simply won't believe it. So, dish them up with whatever you eat at your favourite sushi spot. What about Udon Salad with Sashimi Tuna (p. 54) or Hamachi Tartare (p. 104).

JERK CHICKEN STIR-FRY:
Irie, Mr. Chan, Mon

Serves 4

Spicy jerk chicken takes me back to vacation days fuelled by Red Stripe beer, Caribbean breezes and sandy rubdowns in a tropical paradise. Jamaican jerk seasoning is a winning combo of peppers, allspice, cinnamon and nutmeg, made even more intriguing when married to another great nationality.

4	skinless, boneless chicken breasts, sliced in strips
1 tbsp	spicy jerk seasoning rub (available at specialty grocery stores)
1 tbsp	vegetable oil
2	garlic cloves, minced
1 tsp	minced fresh ginger
2	carrots, sliced
2	stalks celery, sliced
1	red pepper, sliced
1 cup	drained canned pineapple chunks
1/2 cup	snowpeas, tips removed
5	green onions, sliced in thirds
1/2 cup	beansprouts
1–2 tbsp	soy sauce
1/4 cup	chopped peanuts (optional)

1. Rub chicken slices with jerk seasoning. Cover and marinate for at least 2 hours or overnight in the fridge.
2. Heat oil over high heat in a large wok or frying pan. Swirl it around, then stir-fry chicken strips for 3 minutes. Toss in garlic and ginger; stir-fry a minute more. Remove from wok and set aside.
3. Add carrots, celery, red pepper and pineapple. Stir-fry for 2 minutes. Return chicken to pan. Toss in snowpeas, green onions, beansprouts and soy sauce. Toss together a minute or two more.

TO SERVE:

Sprinkle with peanuts, if using, and side with rice. And have plenty of beer on hand to quench the heat. But above all else, I want you to remember that I shot the sheriff. But I did not shoot the deputy.

HEALTH ALERT
Do not thaw chicken at room temperature. Instead, thaw it slowly in the fridge or more quickly in the microwave on Defrost.

IMPRESSIVE PAELLA:
A Spanish Standard with a Modern Twist

—

Serves 4

1	head garlic
2 tbsp	olive oil plus a drizzle
3 1/2	cups good chicken stock
1/2 tsp	saffron threads
Pinch	sea salt
4	chicken thighs
1 cup	(about 10 oz) sliced chorizo sausage or smoked Cajun-style sausage
1	small onion, minced
1	large red pepper, sliced in strips
1	large tomato, halved, then grated down to skins, peel trashed
2	garlic cloves, sliced
1 1/2 cups	Arborio rice
1 tsp	paprika
1/2 tsp	sea salt
12	fresh large shrimp, peeled and deveined, tails left on
2 tbsp	chopped fresh parsley

This is like risotto with luscious spikings of chicken, spicy sausage, shrimp, roasted garlic and other goodies. It's a bit of a process, but it's worth it. So quit your lollygagging.

1. Preheat oven to 350°F.
2. Lop about 3/4 inch off the top of the garlic bulb. Place on a piece of foil, drizzle with olive oil, wrap foil around garlic to encase and seal, and roast for 40 minutes or until garlic is soft. Set aside. Kick oven temp up to 400°F.
3. In a saucepan, bring the stock to a boil, then reduce to a simmer. In a small measuring cup, crush saffron with salt and grind a bit with a spoon. Stir in 1/2 cup chicken stock and let it steep like tea for a few minutes, then stir into simmering stock. Remove stock from heat.
4. In a 13- or 14-inch ovenproof frying pan (if you don't have a proper paella pan), or two smaller frying pans, heat 2 tbsp olive oil on high heat. Add chicken and sauté until well browned, about 8 minutes. Throw in sausage. Cook another few minutes. Remove meats from pan and set aside. Lower heat to medium-low. Add onion and red pepper to the pan; sauté until softened, about 5 minutes. Add tomato and sliced garlic; cook for another 10 minutes.

5. Add rice to pan and stir around so that all the grains get coated with oil and juices. Add paprika and salt, stir to combine, then evenly distribute vegetables, chicken and sausage around the pan. Pat rice down in an even layer so it blankets the bottom of the dish. Kick heat up to medium-high and pour in 3 cups of the chicken stock. Put roasted head of garlic in middle. Don't stir a thing. Bring to a boil, then put uncovered pan in oven for 20 minutes or until rice is tender and no liquid is left. If it's *not* done and there is no liquid left, pour in remaining 1/2 cup of stock and pop it back in the oven.

6. Just before you're ready to take paella out of the oven, quickly sauté the shrimp in a drizzle of olive oil until they turn pink. Sprinkle with a bit of salt and pepper and add to paella when it's finished.

TO SERVE:

Fluff the rice with a fork, sprinkle with parsley and bring 'er over to the table. Warn your guests that the pan is piping hot, but let people serve themselves, making sure to scrape up the yummy crispy bits from the top and bottom and to take a squeeze of roasted garlic as a condiment. You've really outdone yourself!

PAVLOVA
A Crisp and Fluffy Kiwi Concoction

Serves 8–10

2	egg whites, at room temperature
1/2 tsp	vanilla
Pinch	salt (helps to stabilize meringue)
2/3 cup	sugar
3	kiwifruit and 1 mango (or other tropical fruit that can be finely diced to make fruit confetti)
2 cups	whipping cream
1	passion fruit

A meringue shell, sultry whipped cream and a colourful confetti of tropical fruit. This dish may have been invented in New Zealand, but the first time I had it was at a fly-in fishing lodge in the heart of the Yukon's Ruby Range. Chef José Janssen finished off her fab Thai meal with this sweet dessert. Working off a palette of worldly influences, she also had the first tandoori oven north of 60.

1. Preheat oven to 300°F. Draw a 10-inch circle on a piece of wax or parchment paper and place, writing-side down, on a cookie sheet.
2. With an electric beater, beat egg whites with vanilla and salt until they form soft peaks (hint: they fold over on themselves). Then add sugar, about a tablespoon at a time, beating on high until they form stiff peaks (hint: they no longer fold over on themselves) and sugar is dissolved. This will take a few minutes.
3. Tip meringue into circle on cookie sheet, and using the back of a spoon, spread it into a circle, gently building up the sides to form a bowl-like vessel.
4. Bake for 35 minutes. Turn off the oven and let meringue dry in oven with the door closed for 1

hour. No peeking. When time's up, remove the shell from cookie sheet and carefully peel off wax paper. Knock on it carefully; it will sound hollow.

5. Cut kiwifruit and mango into small perfect dice. Whip cream into soft peaks.

TO SERVE:

Just before serving, fill meringue bowl with whipped cream and sprinkle with a colourful dose of fruit confetti. Scoop passion fruit seeds and some juice on top. Dessert as celebration.

INTERNATIONAL THIRST-QUENCHERS
Exotic Tipples
Each drink serves 1

From sweet to potent to alcohol-free, adding a culture-appropriate drink to your bridge-building meal is always a welcome touch.

INDIAN MANGO LASSI

1 cup plain yogurt
2 tsp sugar
1/4 cup cubed mango
3 tbsp ice water
2 tbsp milk

Add all ingredients to a blender with a few ice cubes and whiz until smooth.

SINGAPORE SLING

2 oz gin
1 oz cherry brandy
Juice of 1/2 lemon
Dash of Benedictine
Club soda
Mint sprig

To a martini shaker two-thirds full of crushed ice, add the gin, cherry brandy, lemon juice and Benedictine. Shake hard, then strain into a chilled highball glass. Top with club soda and garnish with a sprig of mint.

MOJITO

2 oz white rum (Cuban would be apropos)
5 fresh mint leaves, torn in half
1/2 tsp sugar
Dash of Angostura bitters

Put all ingredients in a martini shaker two-thirds full of crushed ice. Shake hard and pour into a chilled tumbler.

THEY'RE HERE,
THEY'RE HUNGRY AND THEY WON'T LEAVE:
Quick fixes for drop-by guests

Just because they're annoying doesn't mean you still don't want to dazzle; remember, this is all about you, not them. And this is also where that well-stocked pantry of yours will come in handy. (Note to self: order Call Display.)

ANTIPASTO PLATTER:
A Heaping Plate of Bling Bling

Serves 4–6

1	small eggplant, cut in very thin rounds
2 tbsp plus 1 tsp	olive oil
	Salt and pepper
6	breadsticks
1 tbsp	honey
6	thin slices prosciutto
6	pitted dates
3 tsp	mascarpone or soft cream cheese
	Small bunch of fresh basil
	A couple of handfuls spiced mixed olives (from the deli)
	A few bottled roasted red peppers, drained and sliced in strips
1 jar	(6 oz) marinated artichoke hearts, drained
1	large mango, peeled and sliced

I like to serve this platter during *Sopranos* night at my place.

1. Preheat broiler.
2. Brush eggplant slices on both sides with 2 tbsp of the oil and sprinkle with salt and pepper. Arrange eggplant on a cookie sheet and broil on one side until golden. Flip and do likewise for the other side. Set aside.
3. Spread each breadstick with honey, leaving a couple of inches clean at one end for holding, then tightly wrap a slice of prosciutto around the honey. You have essentially created meat lollipops. Congrats!
4. Open up the dates and stuff each one with 1/2 tsp mascarpone.

TO SERVE:

Now it's time to make this platter of sweet and savoury goodness look like a million bucks. Mound the eggplant up in one corner. Stick the basil beside it and drizzle with 1 tsp olive oil. Arrange the breadsticks in a rustic pile. Put the stuffed dates beside them. Over at the other end, the olives, artichokes and peppers get their own little piles. Stick the mango slices towards the middle. It's all colourful, gorgeous and edible. What more could your guests ask for?

APPLE AND CELERY DIJONNAISE:
A Saucy Little Salad

A 21st-century spin on the Waldorf salad. Back to the future.

1. In a large bowl, whisk together mayo, mustard, vinegar, sugar, salt and pepper. Taste to make sure it's appropriately yummy. Add celery, apples, pecans and parsley. Toss together.

TO SERVE:

Lay a couple of lettuce leaves on each of four salad plates, then scoop a nice serving of the salad onto each. Top with a dose of blue cheese.

2 tbsp	mayonnaise
1 tbsp	Dijon mustard
2 tsp	rice vinegar
1/2 tsp	sugar
	Salt and cracked pepper
4	stalks celery, sliced
2	McIntosh or similar apples, sliced in matchsticks
1/4 cup	pecans, toasted and chopped
1 tbsp	chopped fresh parsley
	Boston lettuce leaves
3–4 oz	blue cheese, crumbled

OSTRICH CARPACCIO WITH CHALLAH TOASTS:
Big Bird, Big Taste

—

Serves 6

1	ostrich loin, about 1 lb (available at specialty meat shops)
6	slices challah (a.k.a. egg bread)
2 tbsp	extra virgin olive oil
1 tbsp	freshly squeezed lemon juice
	Salt and cracked pepper
3 oz	Parmesan cheese, shaved with a potato peeler

Hailing from Africa and parts of southwest Asia, ostriches are gigantic flightless birds that can weigh up to 250 pounds and grow to seven feet high. Ostriches have long been raised for their skin, feathers and meat, the latter of which can be compared to very lean beef. It's an intriguing meat that tastes of neither fish nor fowl. Be the first kid on your block to try an exotic meat. Because we all have the very common ingredient of ostrich on hand. But seriously, it freezes beautifully—so why not?

1. Chill ostrich until very cold, at least 3 hours.
2. Preheat oven to 300°F.
3. Cut crusts off bread slices and cut slices into long fingers. Arrange on a baking sheet and toast both sides until lightly browned.
4. Using your sharpest knife, cut ostrich into paper-thin slices (as thin as you can get them). Just before serving, artistically drape ostrich in equal portions over cold salad plates. Drizzle with olive oil and lemon juice. Sprinkle with salt and pepper. Top with Parmesan shavings.

TO SERVE:
Plate the carpaccio à la minute, sided with challah crisps. Then fly it to the table.

MISO:
Soup of the Ages

Serves 4

This wonderfully flavoured broth cradles soft chunks of vegetables and tofu, for an exotic slurp that defies evolution. Prepare all the vegetables and tofu as dictated, and have them standing by so that they're ready for action when called upon.

1 tsp	minced fresh ginger
6	fresh button mushrooms, sliced
1	small onion, diced
1	small carrot, diced
5 oz	soft tofu, cubed
6 cups	water
1/2 cup	miso*
1 tbsp	soy sauce
1/4 tsp	pepper
1 tbsp	mirin (see p. 13)
1 tsp	rice vinegar
1	green onion, chopped (1 tbsp reserved for garnish)

1. In a large soup pot over medium heat, combine ginger, mushrooms, onion and carrot. Stir together for several minutes. Add the tofu, water, miso, soy sauce and pepper. Bring to a boil, reduce heat, cover and simmer for 15 minutes. Just before serving, stir in the mirin, rice vinegar and green onion.

TO SERVE:
Pour a ladle or two of soup into each bowl and sprinkle with chopped green onion.

*Miso is a fermented soy bean paste that comes in a variety of flavours, ranging from mild shiro miso to sweet to dark mugi. I prefer the mild stuff, myself. Look for it in Asian groceries and natural food stores.

RICE PAPER WRAPS WITH PEANUT DIPPING SAUCE:
The Handy Salad

Serves 4

2 oz	bean-thread (cellophane) noodles
3 tbsp	seasoned rice vinegar
8	rounds (8-inch) rice paper
	Boston lettuce leaves, centre ribs removed
2	green onions, cut in 2-inch julienne strips
1/2 cup	julienned tart apples
1/2 cup	shredded carrot
1/3 cup	julienned firm tofu
1/4 cup	fresh mint leaves
1/4 cup	fresh coriander leaves

Peanut Dipping Sauce:

1/4 cup	smooth peanut butter
1/4 cup	warm water
2 tsp	soy sauce
2 tsp	rice vinegar
2 tsp	sesame oil
1	garlic clove, minced
1/2 tsp	chili flakes

Everything from caviar to Cheez-Its can be munched on in the name of an hors d'oeuvre or appetizer. Meant to complement cocktails and stave off hunger, appetizers should court the imagination and give guests a knowing wink as to what may follow. And there's nothing faster than Asian foods for drop-by guests.

1. In a large bowl, cover noodles with hot water and let soak for 20 minutes. Drain well and cut into 3-inch lengths. Return to dried bowl and toss with vinegar.
2. In another large bowl, soak a rice paper round in hot water until pliable, about 1 minute. Carefully (they tear easily) spread out on paper towel, blotting off excess water.
3. Arrange a piece of lettuce leaf on bottom half of round, leaving a 1-inch border along edge. Top lettuce with some green onion, apple, carrot, tofu, noodles and some mint and coriander

leaves. Roll up filling tightly but gently in rice paper, folding in the sides while rolling to make a nice, encased salad roll. Repeat until all rice paper wrappers have been happily stuffed and rolled.

4. To make the dipping sauce, in a small bowl stir together peanut butter and water. At first it will seem like they won't come together, but you can work them into a smooth paste. I know you can! Stir in soy sauce, rice vinegar, sesame oil, garlic and chili flakes until combined.

TO SERVE:

Cut rolls in half on the diagonal and serve with peanut sauce. You'll never eat Thai take out again.

SESAME-CRUSTED SALMON WITH PAN-FRIED SPINACH:
Feast of the Rising Sun

Serves 4

4	salmon fillets, each about 5 oz (also delicious with sea bass when available)
2 tbsp	soy sauce
2 tbsp	mirin (see page 13)
1	piece (1-inch) fresh ginger, peeled and finely chopped
3	garlic cloves, finely chopped
3	green onions, shredded (slice several times length-wise, then chop crosswise)
2 tbsp plus 2 tsp	vegetable oil
2 tbsp plus 1 tsp	hoisin sauce
1/4 cup	toasted sesame seeds (you can buy them already roasted)
1/4 cup	water
2	bunches fresh spinach, washed and chopped in thirds
	Salt and pepper to taste

Moist marinated fillets smeared with rich hoisin sauce and baked in a crust of sesame seeds. They look as good as they taste, and let me tell you: I should only look so good.

1. Rinse and pat dry salmon. In a dish large enough to hold the salmon in one layer, combine soy sauce, mirin, ginger, garlic and green onions. Place salmon in the marinade and turn it to cover all sides. Let it sit for 15 minutes, flipping midway through.

2. Preheat oven to 450°F. Lightly oil a cookie sheet.

3. Heat 2 tbsp of the vegetable oil in a large non-stick frying pan over medium-high heat. Add the salmon (discard the marinade) and fry for 2 minutes on each side. Set aside on a large plate. Using a butter knife, thinly spread the top and sides of each fillet with 2 tbsp of the hoisin sauce. Pat about 1 tbsp of the sesame seeds onto the top of each piece of fish. Place the fillets on the cookie sheet and bake for 4 minutes.

4. While the fish is baking, stir remaining 1 tsp hoisin sauce into 1/4 cup water. Wipe out the frying pan and heat remaining 2 tsp oil over medium heat. Add spinach and stir-fry for 2 minutes. Pour hoisin mixture over spinach. Cook for another minute. Drain spinach.

TO SERVE:

Place the spinach on a serving plate and lay your beautiful salmon fillets on top. Side it with a bowl of steamed rice.

LEMON RISOTTO WITH SEARED SEA SCALLOPS:
The Old Man and the Rice

—

Serves 4

Risotto:

4 cups	vegetable or chicken stock
2 tbsp	unsalted butter
1 tsp	olive oil
2	garlic cloves, minced
3	large shallots, minced
1 1/2 cups	Arborio rice
1/4 cup	dry white wine or vermouth
1/4 cup	grated or shaved Parmesan cheese
1 1/2 tsp	lemon zest
1 tbsp	olive oil
8	extra-large sea scallops (fresh dry-packed are best as they don't ooze liquid)
	Salt and pepper to taste
	Parsley sprigs, for garnish (optional, but nice)

It's fancy, it's foolproof, and I christened myself a culinary genius the first time I made it. (Modesty is not my strongest suit.) If you're as lazy as I am, instead of simmering stock, just boil water in a kettle and make the stock in a 4-cup measuring cup right as you begin. It'll stay hot enough for the next 20 minutes.

1. To make the risotto, bring stock to a simmer. In a large, heavy saucepan over medium heat, heat butter and oil. Add garlic and shallots. Cook, stirring, for a few minutes until shallots are soft.
2. Stir in rice, coating with butter mixture. Reduce heat to medium-low. Add 1 cup of hot stock and stir until it is absorbed. Keep adding stock, about 1/2 cup at a time, stirring and letting the stock absorb each time, until all the stock has been used and the risotto is tender and creamy. Stir, stir, stir! From start to finish, this process will take about 20 minutes.
3. Meanwhile, preheat oven to 450°F.
4. Stir wine, Parmesan and zest into risotto. Add an extra knob of butter when everyone's looking, just to show them who's boss around here. Remove from heat and keep warm.
5. In a large ovenproof frying pan, heat 1 tbsp oil over high heat. Pat scallops dry. Arrange a few

scallops in the pan, flat side down. Cook till a golden crust forms, about 30 seconds, then flip and sear the other side so that it too has an admirable crust. Remove seared scallops from the pan and repeat with remaining scallops. When all scallops have been seared, put them back in the pan, season with salt and pepper, transfer pan to oven and finish cooking for 5 to 7 minutes or until they firm up (with some give).

TO SERVE:

Dish it up while it's hot. Top each mound of risotto with a couple of scallops and a shaving of Parmesan. And a sprig of parsley. And a flourish of fresh pepper grindings.

COOKING TIP
Stir risotto with a wooden spoon. It cuts back on rice breakage, for which Uncle Luigi is sure to say, "Grazie."
BONUS USE:
Crack the spoon over people's knuckles if they get underfoot.

DULCE DE LECHE:
The Magic Can Dessert

—

Serves 6

1	can (300ml) sweetened condensed milk* Your choice of sturdy fresh fruit, sliced (apples, bananas, oranges, pears)

In South American countries this caramel-like sauce is a key ingredient in delectable cakes, flans, cookies, ice cream . . . just about any sweet dessert. It's best on its own though, either scooped by the spoonful into mouth or as a warm dip for fresh fruit. Surprisingly, the fruit doesn't ruin it. I always have a bowl of this at the ready in the fridge.

1. Get a big pot, put the unopened can in the middle and fill the pot with water, covering the can by at least an inch of water. Bring to a boil, reduce heat and simmer for 2 1/2 hours, making sure the can is always covered with water. Remove from water and let cool completely before opening can.

*There's a warning on the can of sweetened condensed milk that says never heat an unopened can. Warnings are for suckers. Alternatively, you can pour it out of the can and into a covered large microwave-safe bowl and zap for 5 minutes on High.

TO SERVE:

The dulce de leche will be a bit stiff. If you want to make it runnier, spoon it into a bowl, give it a good stir, and heat it up in the microwave for about 20 seconds. Pour into a bowl surrounded by sliced fresh fruit. Also great poured over ice cream.

DRINKS TIP

If friends have surprised you by showing up for dinner and didn't even have the common decency to bring wine, well, I don't know what to say. Just serve tap water. They'll get the point. However, if you happen to be the non-vindictive sort, this is where a well-stocked wine cellar and bar come in handy. Crack open the Baby Duck!

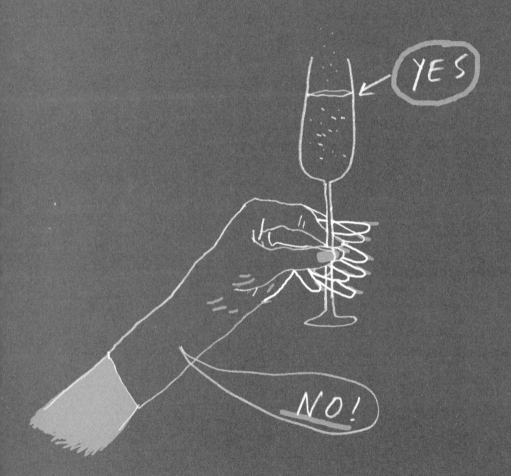

IT'S JUST US CHICKS:
Teatime dainties

Most historians agree that it was Queen Catherine, the wife of Charles II, who introduced tea as a social habit to English high society in 1662. She insisted that a formal tea should be served every afternoon at precisely three o'clock. She would invite several ladies of her court to these teas, whereupon a goodly variety of cakes and biscuits would be servant-served. The women were expected to dress as formally as if they were attending a state dinner. Frilly doilies, upturned noses and radish roses not your cuppa tea? Read on. This is the new-school way to throw a tea party. And I can guarantee that Queen Catherine would most definitely not approve.

ENDIVE STUFFED WITH FAUX CRAB:
Lettuce Be Fairweather Friends

—

Serves 8–10

1	ear corn (or 1/2 cup frozen niblets)
4	Belgian endives (buy firm white ones with a pale yellow tip)
1	pkg fake crab legs, finely chopped
	Juice of 1 lime
2 tbsp	good mayonnaise
2 tsp	sugar
1/4 tsp	salt
1/4 tsp	chili flakes
2	green onions, chopped
2 tbsp	chopped fresh coriander, plus extra for garnish

A delicate mixture of crisp endive cups filled with a zippy mélange of sweet crabmeat and grilled corn. So this is how the other half lives.

1. Scrape corn from cob. In a dry pan over high heat, cook corn, stirring constantly, until it blackens slightly. Season with salt to taste. Transfer to a medium bowl and let cool.

2. Carefully remove endive leaves by slicing off the very bottom of the heads and then pulling the leaves away. Rinse and pat dry. Set aside.

3. To bowl with corn, add crabmeat, lime juice, mayo, sugar, salt, chili flakes, green onions and coriander. Mix well and taste for seasoning.

4. Place a spoonful of the mixture in each endive leaf, pressing it down slightly with the spoon so it spreads from end to end. Cover and refrigerate until serving.

GREENGROCER TIP
Belgian endive can usually be found year round, although their peak season is from November through April. They should be kept in the fridge, wrapped in damp paper towel inside a plastic bag. Once exposed to light, they become bitter, so don't take them for a walk at high noon.

TO SERVE:

These cool, bite-sized morsels look mighty pretty when arranged in a spiral, with an extra sprinkle of coriander on top.

KOSHER NOTE

Not all brands of artificial crabmeat, also known as "sea legs," are kosher. The ones that are will be clearly labelled thus, with the symbols U (the certification of the Union of Orthodox Rabbis) or K, another widespread kosher symbol. Sometimes P is used, denoting certification for pareve (okay for meals that are neither dairy- nor meat-based). Listen, kashrut is confusing at the best of times, so when you start getting into imitation unkosher foods, things get really tricky. But you do get to brush up on the alphabet.

TEA SANDWICHES:
For Alice in Wonderland Types

—

Each recipe makes 16 small sandwiches

The long-heralded return of the proper British tea is finally upon us, and one of the greatest pleasures of any tea party is consuming the vast amount of mini sandwiches that are served. When making such sandwiches, be mindful that the bread should be sliced thinly and served without crusts (a serrated bread knife works best). The sandwich should be large enough for only two bites and cut in thin rectangles, triangles, rounds or squares. And of course the best part: you can eat as many as you want and it still amounts to one sandwich in the eyes of the tea party gods. Now go forth and make these tea treats, my loyal subjects.

CUCUMBER, RADISH AND TARRAGON BUTTER SANDWICHES

1/4 cup	unsalted butter, softened
2 tbsp	minced fresh tarragon
1/4 tsp	sea salt
	Cracked pepper
8	slices whole wheat bread, crusts trimmed off
1/2	English cucumber, peeled and sliced paper thin
3	radishes, sliced paper thin

1. In a small bowl, combine butter, tarragon, salt and pepper. Mix well.
2. Spread tarragon butter on one side of each bread slice, all the way to the edges. Lay the cucumber and radish on four of the slices. Top with the remaining bread, pressing down gently, to make four sandwiches. Cut diagonally into quarters.

1/2 cup	cream cheese, softened
1/4 cup	sliced pitted green olives
1/4 cup	chopped toasted walnuts
Dash	Tabasco sauce
	Cracked pepper to taste
8	slices whole wheat bread, crusts trimmed off

CREAM CHEESE, OLIVE AND WALNUT SANDWICHES

1. In a small bowl, combine cream cheese, olives, walnuts, Tabasco and pepper. Mix well.
2. Spread 2 tbsp cheese mixture on four slices of the bread, then top with remaining slices to make four sandwiches. Cut diagonally into quarters.

1/4 cup	unsalted butter, softened
1 tbsp	snipped chives
1 tsp	lemon zest
1/4 tsp	sea salt
8	slices thin white bread, crusts trimmed off
1 cup	watercress leaves

WATERCRESS AND LEMON BUTTER SANDWICHES

1. In a small bowl, combine butter, chives, zest and salt. Mix well.
2. Spread the butter on one side of each bread slice. Lay the watercress on four of the slices. Top with the remaining bread to make four sandwiches. Cut diagonally into quarters.

OUTDOORSY TIP
Save the crusts.
Feed the birds.

AVOCADO SOUP:
It *Is* Easy Being Green

—

Serves 4

2	avocados
1 cup	half-and-half cream
3/4 cup	vegetable or chicken stock, at room temperature
2	green onions, minced
	Zest and juice of 1 large lime
2 tbsp	fresh chopped coriander
1/2 tsp	sugar
1/4 tsp	salt
	Pepper to taste

Songs about rainbows and cute Muppets notwithstanding, don't try sticking your hand in it to make it talk. That's just a waste of great soup.

1. Cut avocados in half lengthwise, remove pits, scoop out flesh and put in a bowl. Add cream, stock, green onions, lime zest and juice, coriander, sugar, salt and pepper. Blitz with a hand blender until smooth. Taste and adjust seasoning. Cover with plastic wrap touching the surface. (Avocados discolour like crazy and the soup will turn an unappetizing shade of brown if you don't protect it thusly.) Chill for at least an hour.

TO SERVE:
Ladle soup out in small bowls and sprinkle with more chopped coriander, if you please.

JICAMA ORANGE SALAD WITH CHIVE OIL:
Like a Bite of Sunshine

Crunchy and sweet, colourful and pretty, packed with flavour and vitamin C. The cruelness of winter is defenceless against the power of the citrus salad.

1	small jicama, peeled
2	large seedless oranges, peels sliced off with bitter white pith
1/2 cup	chives
1/2 cup	olive oil
1 tbsp	fresh lime juice
1/2 tsp	sea salt
	Cracked pepper
Pinch	sugar
1/4 cup	toasted slivered almonds, for garnish
	Edible flowers, for garnish (optional)

1. Cut jicama in half lengthwise, then cut halves into quarters and thinly slice. Cut oranges into thin rounds, then quarter rounds.
2. Chop up the chives, stick in a blender and pour in olive oil. Blend until brilliant green and smooth with just a few flecks of chive. Put in fridge.
3. On a nice platter, toss together jicama and orange slices. Sprinkle with lime juice, salt, pepper and sugar. Chill for about 20 minutes.
4. Strain chive blender mix through a fine sieve or cheesecloth and you've got yourself some vibrant chive oil drizzle.

TO SERVE:

Give jicama and orange slices another quick toss, then drizzle with chive oil. Sprinkle with toasted almonds and edible flowers (available at gourmet groceries) if you're feeling extra girlish.

LOOKS LIKE DRIZZLE

CRUNCHY ASIAN SLAW:
Barney's Purple "I Love You" Salad

—

Serves 8–10

1/2 cup	slivered almonds
1	pkg ramen noodles, crushed in their bag, seasoning packet set aside for a rainy-day project
1/2	small head red cabbage, finely shredded
1 cup	broccoli florets
1/4	red onion, finely sliced
1/2 cup	snowpeas, tipped and cut in half
1 cup	beansprouts

Dressing:

1/4 cup	rice vinegar
1/4 cup	vegetable oil
1 tbsp	good runny honey
2 tsp	soy sauce
1 tsp	minced fresh ginger
1 tsp	sesame oil
Pinch	chili flakes

This salad has turned up at every potluck I've been to over the past decade. I never get sick of it because everyone's version is different. Plus, equally healthy and yummy.

1. Preheat oven to 400°F.
2. Place almonds and crushed ramen noodles on a cookie sheet and toast for a few minutes until lightly browned. Set aside to cool.
3. Place prepared veggies in a salad bowl. Cover and chill.
4. Using a blender or a bowl and whisk, blend together vinegar, vegetable oil, honey, soy sauce, ginger, sesame oil and chili flakes until emulsified. Adjust seasoning to suit your taste.

TO SERVE:
Drizzle, taste, toss and go.

SNOWPEAS WITH WASABI CREAM CHEESE AND GINGER:
Crudité Nirvana

Makes about 2 dozen

25–30	snowpeas, woody tips peeled away
4 oz	cream cheese, softened
4 tsp	wasabi paste (if you have powder, mix it into a paste)
2 tbsp	vegetable oil
1	piece (2 inches) ginger, peeled and coarsely grated, juice squeezed out through paper towel
Pinch	salt

I'm ashamed to admit that I got this idea from Martha S. But you've just gotta know that she stole it from some put-upon caterer as she was ritzing it up in an underdeveloped country. I've added my own touch and now I'm handing the recipe to you. Pay the snowpeas forward.

1. To take the raw taste out of the snowpeas, put a small pot of water on to boil, then blanch the snowpeas (read: quick-cook them in boiling water for just a minute). Drain in a colander and chill with cold running water to stop the cooking. Put in fridge.

2. In a small bowl, mix together cream cheese and wasabi paste until smooth. Cover and refrigerate.

3. Heat oil in a small frying pan over medium-high heat. Sprinkle in ginger and stir around until golden brown. Drain on paper towel. Dust with a pinch o' salt.

COOKING TIP
The easiest way to peel ginger is with the tip of a spoon. Just scrape down with a bit of force. No waste, and you get to keep all of your fingers.

TO SERVE:
Fill a piping bag (or a sandwich baggy with a corner snipped off) with cream cheese mixture and pipe a line over each snowpea. Top with a sprinkle of fried ginger. Line them up on a plate and hand them out. Dainty little devils.

BAKED TRIPLE-STRAWBERRY CHEESECAKE:
A Cake, Its Fruit, the Sauce and Her Lover

—

Serves 8–10

2 cups	graham cracker crumbs
5 tbsp	butter, melted
3	pkg (each 8 oz) cream cheese (not low-fat, nor whipped, please)
3/4 cup	sugar
3	eggs
2 tbsp	fresh lemon juice
1 tsp	lemon zest
1 tsp	vanilla
2 cups	strawberries, hulled and halved, at room temperature, divided Double-dipped strawberries (p. 218), for garnish (optional)

Strawberry Sauce:

2 cups	strawberries, hulled and chopped
3 tbsp	sugar
1 tbsp	fresh lemon juice

A rich cream cheese filling with berries in the mix, as a sauce, fresh on top and dipped on the side. For the strawberry masochist in us all.

1. Preheat oven to 325°F. Spray a 9-inch spring-form pan with nonstick cooking spray (or use a nonstick pan).

2. Stir together graham crumbs and melted butter. Press into bottom of springform pan. Bake crust for 10 minutes. Let cool on a rack.

3. In a large bowl, beat together cream cheese and sugar until sugar dissolves. Add eggs one at a time, and beat in until combined. Stir in lemon juice, lemon zest and vanilla. Stir in 1 cup of the strawberries.

4. Pour mixture into cooled crust and bake for 45 minutes or until centre is almost set—just slightly jiggly. Let cool on a rack, then refrigerate for at least 2 hours or the whole day if you're getting your roots touched up.

5. To make the strawberry sauce (a.k.a. coulis), plop strawberries into a blender, add sugar and lemon juice, and purée. (This can also be done with a hand blender.)

TO SERVE:

Run a knife around the edge of the cake and remove sides of pan. Slice cheesecake with a wet knife for clean wedges. Spoon some strawberry sauce over top and add a sprinkling of remaining 1 cup halved strawberries. Side with a big fat chocolate-dipped berry, if you went that extra mile.

STYLE TIP
How to Buy a Hat

If you're throwing a tea party, you should come in full regalia, and that includes a proper hat. However, since nobody has worn one since a slight surge in popularity following Molly Ringwald's teen-angst turn in *Sixteen Candles*, you probably don't own one. Here are a few simple rules for successful purchasing.

1) A hat should be worn straight across the forehead, just above the eyebrows and with the tips of the ears tucked in.
2) It should not move around when placed on straight, or leave a mark on your forehead when you remove it.
3) Short? Avoid a wide-brimmed hat, as people will not see beyond it.
4) Four eyes? Choose a hat with an upbrim so as not to cover your glasses.
5) As for colour, yellow tones and greys are hard to wear around the face in winter, but pink looks pretty on most gals.

LEMON CURD IN SHORTBREAD TARTS:
Pucker Up, Buttercup

—

Makes 12 tarts

Tart shells:

1 cup	unsalted butter, softened
1/2 cup	brown sugar
1/2 tsp	vanilla
2 1/4 cups	all-purpose flour

Lemon Curd:

4	egg yolks
1	egg
1 cup	sugar
1/2 cup	fresh lemon juice (about 3 lemons)
1/2 cup	unsalted butter, at room temperature

Raspberries, for garnish (optional, but yummy and pretty)

The buttery texture of the pastry coupled with the tangy sweetness of the lemon curd borders on sensory overload. You'll have to sit down to eat these.

1. Preheat oven to 325°F.

2. To make the shortbread tart shells, in a medium bowl, cream together butter and brown sugar until light and fluffy. Stir in vanilla, then gradually mix in flour. The dough should eventually make itself into a big proud ball. If it's still sticky, mix in a bit more flour, a tablespoon at a time, but be careful not to overwork the dough.

3. Using a rolling pin, wine bottle or whatever you have handy, roll out the dough on a lightly floured surface so that it's about 1/4 inch thick but still manageable. Cut the dough into twelve 3-inch rounds (use a cookie cutter or the top of a drinking glass), then press the rounds into muffin tins. Poke the bottoms with a fork a couple of times.

4. Bake for 15 minutes or until lightly browned. Cool on a wire rack, then pop out tart shells.

5. Now for the curd. In a medium saucepan over low heat, whisk together egg yolks, whole egg, sugar and lemon juice for 10 minutes or until mixture thickens. You'll know when this happens. But if you're still unsure of your culinary prowess in the kitchen, make sure the mixture

coats the back of a spoon. Then you're golden. But not done yet. Remove pot from heat and stir in the butter, a little pat at a time, until it's all done and you're in lemon heaven. Let it cool and thicken up, stirring it every so often.

TO SERVE:

Fill the cooled shortbread shells with cooled lemon curd and top with a few raspberries. Well, look at you, Miss Baker thang.

THREE QUICK TIPS
FOR BECOMING
A BETTER BAKER:
1. Always preheat the oven.
2. Never use imitation
vanilla extract.
3. Lick the spoon.

MIMOSA:
Kicking Orange Juice

—

Serves 4–8, depending on thirst

1	bottle (750 mL) good-quality champagne or sparkling wine, chilled
8 cups	fresh-squeezed or non-reconstituted-style orange juice, chilled

This brunchtime specialty is as simple to make as O.J. + champagne. End result—a delectable drink, and a pleasant noontime buzz.

1. Stir together both liquids in a big glass jug.

TO SERVE:

Fill spotless champagne flutes to the three-quarters mark. Passing the glasses out from a drink-filled tray is always a nice, hospitable touch.

TEA PARTY TIPS
Yes to dainty sandwiches, no to white kid leather gloves. Yes to fresh flowers and lovely sweets, no to carob anything. Yes to fun cocktails, yes to more fun cocktails.

Pink is the biggest girlhood cliché. Instead of denying it, own it.

PINK ELEPHANT

To a martini shaker two-thirds full of ice, add bourbon, lemon juice, grenadine and egg white. Shake hard, then pour into a chilled cocktail glass.

2 oz	bourbon
1 oz	fresh lemon juice
2 dashes	grenadine
1	egg white

PINK LADY

To a martini shaker two-thirds full of ice, add gin, apple brandy, lime juice, egg white and grenadine. Shake vigorously, then strain into a chilled cocktail glass.

1 oz	gin
1/2 oz	apple brandy
	Juice of 1/2 lime
1	egg white
Dash	grenadine

PINK PANTHER

To a martini shaker two-thirds full of ice, add Pernod and grenadine. Shake valiantly, pour into a highball glass and top with club soda.

2 oz	Pernod
Dash	grenadine
	Club soda

YOUR ROOTS ARE SHOWING:
Lo-Fi cooking for trailer-trash treats

Mostly down-home vittles and quick good eats here. Some retro favourites and nostalgia treats too. It's all good stuff, and it's always there for you, just like home. Just like beer. Just like the trailer park.

WHITE-TRASH BEEFBURGERS:
Varmint and Toppings

—

Serves 4

1 1/2 lb	lean ground chuck
1/2 tsp	kosher salt
	A few grinds of
	cracked pepper
4	hamburger buns

Fancy-pants city-folk toppings:

Sautéed mushrooms

Arugula

Caramelized onions

Crumbled blue cheese

Roasted red peppers

Sharp Cheddar

Horseradish

Aïoli

Mango chutney

Trash toppings:

Peanut butter (think Elvis)

Coleslaw (it works)

Fried egg and bacon (don't think about your heart!)

Grilled salami (with yellow mustard, of course)

Kraft Singles (a perennial fave) or a
   spritz of cheese-in-a-can (even classier)

Pineapple rings (best when grilled)

The car is up on cinder blocks, you've polished off another two-four, the gang is coming over and it's your turn to cook. There's no denying that burgers are everyone's favourite. So suck in that beer gut and start grilling these perfect burgers. Have the regular bottled condiments, plus pickles, tomatoes, lettuce and onions on hand. And why not add some optional toppings for those who dare to express their inner burger?

1. Preheat grill to medium.
2. Shape chuck into four burgers, about 3/4 inch thick, and season both sides with salt and pepper. Grill until crispy on the outside and juicy on the inside, about 8 minutes, flipping just once halfway through cooking. A meat thermometer should read 160°F.
3. Toast the buns while you're at it.

TO SERVE:

Put out the burgers and condiments (the more, the more impressive) and feign surprise when everyone goes for the peanut butter.

FIVE RULES FOR SERVING BEER

1. Dead possums taking up all the room in the fridge? Store your brew in a cool, dark place, but don't keep it in the freezer. It will go cloudy and flat, if it doesn't explode.
2. Don't shake the bottles before serving, unless you feel extreme hostility towards the drinker.
3. Don't serve cans. Not nearly as chic as bottles. Then again, cut-open tins go a long way at repairing punched-in trailer walls.
4. Iced mugs are sexy.
5. If guests opt to use a glass (however unlikely this may be), simply tilt glass and pour beer in on an angle, then straighten towards the end. Makes for good head.

FRIED CHICKEN WITH MASHED TATERS:
Mary-Jo, Lou-Bob and Zeke's Favourite

—

Serves 4

2 tsp	salt
2 cups	water
1	frying chicken (3 to 3 1/2 lb), cut in 8 parts (halved breasts, thighs, drumsticks)
1 1/2 cups	all-purpose flour
2 tsp	seasoning salt (Cajun-style if you have it)
1 tsp	cracked pepper
1 1/2 cups	vegetable shortening

Mashed Potatoes:

4	large potatoes, peeled, each cut in 8 chunks
2 tbsp	butter
1/4 cup	warm milk
1 tsp	salt

Down South they've perfected the art of the fried-chicken dinner. It ain't nothing fancy but sure brings the family round the table in a jiffy—cousins, wives, sister/wives, mother/cousins . . .

1. Dissolve salt in water in a large bowl. Add chicken parts and soak for 20 minutes, then drain.

2. Stir together flour, seasoning salt and pepper. Dredge chicken parts in seasoned flour until well coated.

3. Over medium heat (in a cast-iron frying pan if you have one), melt shortening and heat to about 350°F. Cook the chicken, a few pieces at a time, until browned on all sides and cooked through, about 20 minutes. (Alternatively, brown it in the pan and finish it off on a cookie sheet in a 350°F oven.) Drain on paper towel. Shake a bit of salt over the hot chicken.

4. Meanwhile, make the taters. Place potatoes in a saucepan and cover with cold water. Bring to a boil, then lower heat and simmer potatoes until a fork glides through them, 15 to 20 minutes.

5. Drain in a colander, plop potatoes back in the pot and mash with a potato masher or a big fork. Stir in butter till it melts, then add warm milk, salt and pepper to taste. Heat on low for a couple of minutes.

TO SERVE:

A plate of chicken, a bowl of potatoes, and why not cook up some collard greens while you're at it? I wouldn't say no to Wet Naps either. The South shall rise again! (After dinner.)

HOW TO DO TRAILER LIVIN' RIGHT

Should you happen to find yourself living in a trailer, take some time to learn how to do it right. Fire up the TV and study '70s reruns of Jim Rockford, slick private dick on *The Rockford Files*. Despite his cramped living quarters on wheels, he was never in want of anything, and always looked groomed, well rested and well fed. Lesson learned? Trailer living *can* be glamorous.

TEMPURA ONION RINGS:
Burger King Has Nothing on the Japanese

—

Serves 4

Tempura:

1 cup	ice-cold soda water
1 cup plus 1/4 cup	cake flour
	Vegetable oil for frying
2	sweet Vidalia or white Spanish onions, sliced in even 1/2-inch rings
1/2 tsp	sea salt

Dipping Sauce:

1/4 cup	soy sauce
1/4 cup	mirin (see p. 13)
1 tsp	wasabi paste (optional)

Who knew tempura was so easy? What the hell are they trying to pull? Mama didn't raise no fool.

1. To make the tempura, in a large bowl whisk together soda water and 1 cup of the flour until almost smooth; a few lumps are actually desirable in tempura.

2. Pour about 3 inches of vegetable oil into a wok or large, deep frying pan. Heat it to about 375°F.

3. Dredge onion rings in remaining 1/4 cup cake flour, patting off the excess. Dip each ring in tempura batter, shake off excess, and gently drop into the hot oil, a few at a time. Fry for a couple of minutes, flipping halfway through, until the coating is slightly browned and crunchy and the onion is soft. Drain on paper towel and sprinkle with salt.

4. To make the dipping sauce, stir together soy sauce, mirin and wasabi paste, if using.

TO SERVE:

Make these at the last minute so that they're piping hot, to the point that your guests are eating them while you're frying up batches (a soggy tempura is a sad tempura). Set out the bowl of dipping sauce and let them go at it. I won't be happy unless everybody burns his or her tongue. I mean it.

BBQ BEEF SPARERIBS:
Put Some Meat on Them Bones

Serves 6

If someone makes you ribs, it's a sure sign that they love you. They're trying to make you happy. So will you do me a favour? Try to be a little nicer to them. They're reaching out. It wouldn't kill you.

1. Preheat oven to 350°F.
2. In a large frying pan, heat oil over medium heat. Brown ribs in hot oil. Transfer ribs to a large baking dish. Combine sugar, soy sauce, water, W-sauce, mustard and garlic; toss with ribs. Cover and bake for 2 hours. Remove cover and cook another 30 minutes or until browned and tender.

TO SERVE:

Finger bowls and napkins are in order. And don't quote me on this, but I'm thinking rice.

3 tbsp	vegetable oil
3 lb	thick-cut beef short ribs (a.k.a. Miami ribs)
1/2 cup	brown sugar
1/2 cup	soy sauce
1/2 cup	water
1 tbsp	Worcestershire sauce
1 tsp	mustard powder
3	garlic cloves, minced

SWEET CORN FRITTERS WITH BACON AND SYRUP:
Better Than It Sounds

—

Serves 4

2	eggs, separated
2 cups	fresh, frozen or canned corn (fresh is best, but we don't judge here)
1	green onion, white part only, minced
2 tbsp	all-purpose flour
1/2 tsp	salt
	Cracked pepper
	Butter or margarine for frying
8	slices bacon
	Maple syrup

A Mennonite specialty for fuelling days filled with barn-raisings and quilting bees. Or coon shootin'. Whichever.

1. Beat egg yolks in a bowl. Add corn, green onion, flour, salt and pepper. Stir together.
2. In another bowl, beat egg whites until stiff peaks form. This takes a couple of minutes but it's a great stress reliever, and turning liquid into a semisolid makes you feel like a million bucks. Gently but thoroughly fold egg whites into the corn batter.
3. Melt some butter in a large nonstick frying pan over medium-high heat. Drop tablespoonfuls of batter into the bubbling butter.
4. Brown, then flip. Brown, then flip. If you're a good multi-tasker, you should be cooking the bacon in another pan right about now. If you're not, keep the finished fritters warm in a preheated 200°F oven and go cook that damn bacon.

TO SERVE:

A few little fritters on each plate topped with a couple of bacon strips and a drizzle of maple syrup. Life is good.

PASSING THOUGHT
Is it just me, or is bacon the candy of the meat world?

Serves 6–8

These perennial cocktail treats are a favourite of the martini set *and* the juice-cup crowd.

8	good-quality hotdogs
4 cups	biscuit mix (such as Bisquick)
1 cup	milk
1 cup	shredded extra-old Cheddar cheese

1. Preheat oven to 400°F. Spray a cookie sheet with nonstick cooking spray.
2. Cut hotdogs in half crosswise. In a large bowl stir together biscuit mix and milk to form a soft dough. Turn dough out onto a surface lightly dusted with biscuit mix and knead it 10 times.
3. Roll dough into a large, thin rectangle about the size of a cookie sheet and cut into 16 rectangles (finally, those math and geometry skills are coming in handy).
4. Sprinkle some cheese on each rectangle, top with a hotdog half and roll up dough, pinching closed along the seam.
5. Arrange the pigs in blankets on the cookie sheet and bake for 12 to 15 minutes or until the dough is lightly browned and the hotdogs are smelling hot diggity good.

TO SERVE:

Let them cool before handing them out to the chillun. And even though these dogs are mini doesn't mean people won't still want their favourite condiments on hand. You know the drill: mustard, ketchup and relish.

SPAGHETTI AND CHICKEN MEATBALLS:
A Meatball for the New Millennium

Serves 4

1 tbsp	olive oil
1	small onion, chopped
2	garlic cloves, minced
4 cups	tomato sauce (homemade or store-bought)
1 lb	ground chicken
1 cup	dry breadcrumbs
1	egg, beaten
1/2 tsp	ground rosemary
1/2 tsp	salt
	Cracked pepper
1 lb	spaghetti
1/4 cup	minced flat-leaf parsley

Who doesn't love spaghetti and meatballs? Who?! Forget it, I don't want to know these people. Besides, this twist on the familiar favourite is better than good and has less fat and more taste. It's the new-school way to do spag and balls.

1. In a small frying pan, heat olive oil over medium heat. Cook onion and garlic, stirring often, until soft and translucent. Transfer to a bowl and cool.
2. In a large nonstick frying pan, heat 2 cups of the tomato sauce. In the meantime, using your hands, mix together ground chicken, breadcrumbs, egg, rosemary, salt and pepper and cooled onion mixture. Wet hands and form mixture into 16 meatballs.
3. Place balls evenly over heated tomato sauce, then cover with remaining 2 cups sauce. Bring to a simmer, reduce heat to medium-low, cover and cook for 20 minutes or until firm and no longer pink inside. Stir every so often.
4. About halfway through the cooking time, put a pot of salted water on to boil and cook spaghetti until al dente (follow package directions). Drain in a colander.

TO SERVE:

Get out four pasta bowls, divide spaghetti up, top with sauce and chicken balls and a pop of parsley.

BAKED MACARONI AND CHEESE:
KD For Grown-ups

Serves 8 to 10

This is not the same mac and cheese you ate for lunch during grades one through six, while watching *The Flintstones*. And it is not the same mac and cheese that made up your three squares a day at university (while watching *The Simpsons*). It's different. It's better. And I think it's high time you set aside your sour feelings and reconnected with this cheesy friend. Come on, pick up the phone and give old Mac a call.

1 lb	dried elbow macaroni
1/2 cup	unsalted butter, melted
3 cups	2% milk
1 cup	half-and-half cream
1 tbsp	Dijon mustard
1/2	tsp salt
	Cracked pepper
1 lb	sharp Cheddar cheese, shredded

1. Preheat oven to 350°F. Butter a large baking dish.
2. Bring a large pot of water to a boil and cook the macaroni to just about al dente. Drain, shake out excess water and transfer to the baking dish.
3. Toss macaroni with melted butter, covering every elbow, then pour in milk and cream (add more if it doesn't just about cover pasta). Add mustard, salt and pepper. Reserve 1 cup of the cheese for the topping and add remaining cheese to the macaroni. Toss everything together.
4. Bake, uncovered, for 30 to 40 minutes, then give it a stir. When milk and cream is almost all absorbed, turn on broiler, sprinkle top with reserved cheese and broil until the top is nice and browned.

TO SERVE:
Dishing it out while it's hot is a must. Basking in the cheesy glory is optional.

BANANA-SPLIT BREAD PUDDING:
Two Great Desserts That Taste Great Together!

—

Serves 6–8

1	loaf (5–7 oz) stale French bread, crumbled to make 3–4 cups
2 cups	milk
1 cup	sugar
1/4 cup	unsalted butter, melted
1	egg
1	egg yolk
1 tsp	vanilla
1/2 cup	milk chocolate chips
1/2 cup	chopped pecans
1/4 cup	sweetened shredded coconut
1/4 cup	chopped maraschino cherries (plus a handful of whole ones)
1	large banana, sliced
1	canister whipped cream

The first time I visited N'Awleans I took a class at the New Orleans School of Cooking. Through numerous bowls of spicy gumbo and jambalaya, I basically ate my weight in pork fat. But we finished the class with an excellent tropical bread pudding—the inspiration for this kooky concoction. Chef Michael did say to experiment . . .

1. Butter well an 8- by 8-inch baking dish.
2. In a large bowl combine bread, milk, sugar, butter, egg, egg yolk, vanilla, chocolate chips, pecans, coconut, chopped cherries and banana. Mixture should be quite thick and moist, the consistency of your mother's oatmeal. Add a titch more milk if necessary.
3. Pour batter into baking dish, then place in oven. Turn oven on to 350°F and bake until pudding is brown on top and smelling like eternal blessedness, 45 minutes to 1 hour.
4. How easy was that?

TO SERVE:

Let it cool slightly, then cut into large squares, put on plates and squirt with a generous dose of whipped cream. Top with a bright cherry. This calls for some hickory-spiked coffee.

**TIPS FOR SERVING
A BETTER CUP OF JOE**

Use only fresh-roasted, freshly ground coffee. Start with cold, fresh water. Make sure your equipment, from coffee maker to carafe to mugs, is spotless. Measure ingredients carefully, and add a pinch of cinnamon to the grounds for that added *je ne sais quoi*. Have a nice little tray of cold milk and cream, sugar, sweeteners and teaspoons at the ready. Serve it while it's hot.

Good morning

IF YOU LOVE THIS EARTH:
Strictly vegetarian delights

Yes, this sprightly cookery tome has its fair share of meat, fish and poultry recipes, and yes, some of them are even served blood raw. But that's not to say I don't love vegetables, vegetarian food and even vegetarians. Some of my best friends are vegetarians! But enough with the gluey veggie patties and three-bean salads. Here are some delicious high-end meals to prove to your carnivore pals once and for all that eating vegetarian doesn't make you a Birkenstock-wearing, tofu-loving freak. You shall soon emerge as a new and improved Birkenstock-wearing, tofu-loving, gourmet-veggie-cooking freak.

VEGETABLES WITH SALSA VERDE:
Rio del Yummy

Serves 4

2	large potatoes, peeled and cut in 1-inch cubes
2	large carrots, peeled and cut in 1-inch cubes
2	eggs
1	large zucchini, cut into 1-inch cubes
	Chopped fresh parsley, for garnish

Salsa Verde:

3/4 cup	chopped fresh parsley
1	garlic clove, minced
1	large shallot, chopped
4	large pitted green olives, chopped
2 tbsp	fresh lemon juice
1 1/2 tsp	capers, drained and rinsed
1/4 cup	extra virgin olive oil

An easy appetizer from South America and Mexico, where the people are as warm as the midday sun, where boiled vegetables are actually a good thing and where salsa is green. Hey, is it opposite day?

1. Put potatoes, carrots and eggs in a saucepan, cover with salted water, and bring to a low boil. Set the timer for 10 minutes once water begins to boil. In the last 3 minutes, add the zucchini. When time is up, tip contents into a colander and rinse with cold water to stop the cooking.
2. To make the salsa verde, to a blender add parsley, garlic, shallot, olives, lemon juice and capers. Pulse until smooth, then drizzle in olive oil, blending until sauce emulsifies.

TO SERVE:

Peel eggs and slice lengthwise into quarters. Divide cooked vegetables and egg artfully among four salad plates and give each a healthy spooning of sauce. Sprinkle with parsley.

SPRING ONION AND PEA SOUP WITH PISTOU:
Tip-toe Through the Tulips

Serves 4–6

Blossoming buds, Robin Redbreast, chives poking through the soil of your windowsill herb garden, and the smell of dog shit in the air. Ah, spring in the city. Pistou, by the way, is France's answer to herbaceous pesto.

1. In a soup pot, melt butter over medium-high heat. Add green onions and stir around, cooking for a couple of minutes until soft. Add stock and bring to a boil. Add peas, reduce heat to a simmer, cover and cook for 5 minutes.

2. Remove from heat and toss in the mint. Get out your trusty hand blender and purée the soup in the pot until it's smooth. Season with salt and pepper.

3. Make the pistou (the soup is still great without it, by the by). If you have a mortar and pestle, now would be the time to use it, but if not, get out a bowl and spoon and mash together garlic, basil and walnuts until they form a loose paste. Stir in cheese and a little oil, then stir in remaining oil. It won't be emulsified; more like a delectable compound.

1 tbsp	unsalted butter
3	bunches green onions, chopped
4 cups	vegetable stock
3 1/2 cups	thawed frozen peas (or fresh if you can find them)
2 tbsp	chopped fresh mint (or 1 tsp dried)
	Salt and pepper to taste

Pistou:

1	garlic clove, minced
2 tbsp	minced fresh basil
2 tsp	finely chopped walnuts
1 tsp	grated Parmesan cheese
1 tbsp	olive oil

TO SERVE:

Ladle warm soup into bowls and drop a little dollop of pistou into the centre of each. *Très chic.*

OVEN-ROASTED CAPRESE STACKS:
Vertical Baked Salads

—

Serves 6

12	ripe plum tomatoes
1 1/2 tsp	kosher salt
1/2 cup	balsamic vinegar
1	large bunch arugula
4	bocconcini balls (about 2 inches wide), cut in 1/4-inch slices
1 tbsp	olive oil
	Black pepper
	Leaves from 1 large bunch of basil, coarsely chopped

A favourite summer salad gets an up-market makeover. Challenge yourself a little.

1. Preheat oven to 200°F. Line a cookie sheet with foil.
2. Slice stem ends off tomatoes. Cut tomatoes in half lengthwise and scoop out seeds. Put tomatoes on cookie sheet and sprinkle generously with salt. Bake for 2 hours, flipping halfway through.
3. In a small saucepan, bring balsamic vinegar to a boil, then reduce heat and simmer until it reduces by half. Let cool. Reduction will be syrupy.
4. Kick up oven to 300°F. On the cookie sheet, make six stacks of tomato and cheese: start with a tomato half, top it with a slice or two of bocconcini, another tomato half, more cheese, and one more tomato half. Drizzle with a bit of olive oil and give it a crack of black pepper. Bake for 10 minutes or until cheese starts to melt.

TO SERVE:

Put a little mound of chopped basil and arugula on each of six salad plates, then lay a tomato/cheese stack on top. Drizzle the balsamic reduction over and around the stack as artistically as you see fit.

EGGPLANT PARMESAN:
You Don't Like-a da Meatball? You Eat-a da Eggplant

Serves 6

Always remember: Vegetarians are people too.

1	large eggplant, sliced in thin rounds
1 tsp	salt
1 cup	all-purpose flour
2	eggs, beaten
2 cups	seasoned breadcrumbs (Italian-style would be primo)
1/2 cup	vegetable oil (give or take)
3 cups	tomato sauce (store-bought is fine but home-made wins brownie points)
1/2 lb	mozzarella cheese (half a 280 g ball), shredded
1/2 cup	grated Parmesan cheese

1. Put eggplant in a colander and sprinkle with salt; let sit for 1 hour. This helps to leach out the bitterness. Pat dry with paper towel.

2. Preheat oven to 350°F. Set out three bowls: one with flour, one with beaten eggs and one with breadcrumbs. Pour about an inch of oil into a large frying pan and heat over medium-high.

3. Dredge eggplant slices in flour, patting off excess, then dip in egg, then pat into breadcrumbs. Fry both sides of each slice until they're golden brown on the outside and a little soft but not fully cooked on the inside. Drain on paper towel.

4. Spread 1/2 cup of the tomato sauce in a 13- by 9-inch baking dish. Arrange a layer of fried eggplant on top, then spread with 1 cup of sauce. Sprinkle with a good dose of mozzarella and some Parmesan. Repeat layers again, ending with a final thick topping of mozzarella and Parmesan. Bake, uncovered, for 30 to 40 minutes or until everything is hot and bubbly and browned.

TO SERVE:
Let it sit and mellow for about 10 minutes, then slice it up and dish it out.

SWEET POTATO GNOCCHI WITH THREE SAUCE OPTIONS:
Because I'm *All* about Options

—

Serves 4

Gnocchi:

4	medium sweet potatoes
1 cup	all-purpose flour
1/2 cup	dry breadcrumbs
1	egg, lightly beaten
1 tsp	salt
	Cracked pepper

Quick Tomato Sauce:

1/4 cup	olive oil
1	garlic clove, minced
1	can (28 oz) crushed tomatoes
1/2 tsp	sugar
1/4 cup	chopped fresh basil
	Salt and pepper to taste

Speedy Brown Butter and Sage Sauce:

1/2 cup	unsalted butter
2 tbsp	chopped fresh sage
	Salt and pepper to taste

Lickety-split Gorgonzola Cream Sauce:

1/2 cup	whipping cream
1/2 cup	(about 5 oz) cubed Gorgonzola cheese
2 tbsp	dry white wine
	Pepper to taste

So you've decided to make homemade pasta: congratulations! And with this recipe comes your choice of three easy sauces: a quick tomato, speedy brown butter and sage, or lickety-split Gorgonzola. Simply choose the one that best suits your mood. Or your shoes.

1. Preheat oven to 400°F.
2. To make the gnocchi, poke the sweet potatoes several times with a fork. Bake on a cookie sheet until they're soft to the touch, about 45 minutes.
3. When they're cool enough to work with, cut potatoes open and scoop flesh into a bowl. Mash well. Stir in flour and breadcrumbs. Work in egg, then add salt and pepper. Chill for 20 minutes.
4. Put a large pot of salted water on to boil. Get out a glass of warm water, and two teaspoons. Retrieve the gnocchi dough. You, my friend, are about to make quenelles. Sounds scary, but it's so easy. Here's what you do: Using a wet teaspoon, scoop up a little gnocchi dough. (It's wettish, I know.) Using the other wet spoon, scoop the dough from the first spoon in a sweeping, twisting motion. With a bit of practice you should end up with little football-shaped gnocchi. Drop in boiling water about six at a time. They'll float to the

top after a couple of minutes; which means they're done, but cook a minute longer to firm them up. Remove with a slotted spoon and place on a cookie sheet without touching each other. Once they're all cooked, chill gnocchi for 1 hour.

5. When you've made your sauce and you're ready to serve them, bring a large pot of salted water to a boil. Drop gnocchi in in small batches. This is just to reheat them, so take them out after a minute.

FOR SAUCES:

Quick Tomato: Heat oil in a large skillet over medium heat. Add garlic; cook, stirring, for 30 seconds, then stir in crushed tomatoes and sugar. Cook, stirring occasionally, for 10 minutes or until slightly thickened. Add basil, salt and pepper to taste. Done! (P.S. This makes more than you'll need for this recipe.)

Speedy Brown Butter and Sage: In a small saucepan, heat butter until it melts and foams and takes on a slightly nutty colour and scent. Swirl pot a bit as you go, like you're making Jiffy Pop. Remove from heat and stir in sage—careful, because the butter may foam up. Hear it sizzle.

Skim foam off the top, crack in some pepper and a sprinkle of salt. Done!

Lickety-split Gorgonzola Cream: In a medium saucepan, heat cream to just below the boiling point. Add Gorgonzola and whisk until it becomes one with the cream. Pour in wine and heat to just below the boiling point. Simmer for 10 minutes. Add pepper. Done!

TO SERVE:

Serve up the bowl of hot gnocchi and toss with your choice of sauce. A nice little coordinating garnish would be cool too. Some Parmesan shavings with the tomato sauce, a fresh sage leaf with the butter sauce and some chopped parsley on the Gorgonzola.

THAI RED COCONUT TOFU CURRY:
Fire in the Bowl

Serves 4

2 tbsp	vegetable oil
1 lb	extra-firm tofu, cubed and patted dry
2	cans (each 14 oz) unsweetened coconut milk
1	can (14 oz) straw mushrooms, drained
1	can (14 oz) baby corn, drained
1	can (8 oz) sliced water chestnuts, drained
2	stalks lemongrass, root ends cut off and stalks chopped in half (available at Asian markets)
1 tbsp	minced peeled fresh ginger
2	carrots, peeled and sliced
1	red pepper, chopped
1/4 cup	snowpeas
1/4 cup	Thai red curry paste (available in supermarkets or Asian markets)
1 tbsp	sugar
1 tbsp	soy sauce
	Juice of 2 small limes
1/4 cup	chopped fresh coriander

Memories of weeks passed on buttery white sand next to aquamarine water; reading Gabriel García Márquez while being rocked in a hammock by gentle breezes and an Israeli lover. Sun-bleached hair and toasted skin. Nights fuelled by whisky and Coke and full-moon parties on the beach. If you still need to be sold on Thailand, try this coconut curry. Takes me back every time.

1. Heat oil in a large frying pan over medium-high heat. Add dry cubes of tofu and fry until golden on each side, about 5 minutes.

2. Remove pan from heat and reduce heat to medium. In a large saucepan bring coconut milk to a low simmer. Stir in mushrooms, corn, water chestnuts, lemongrass, ginger, carrots, red pepper, snowpeas, curry paste, sugar, soy sauce and golden tofu. Cook for 10 minutes, then stir in lime juice and give her a taste. Too tart? Add more sugar. Not enough heat? More curry paste. Not salty enough? More soy sauce. Thai food is a fine balancing act, and you'll know when you've got it right.

TO SERVE:

Discard lemongrass, pour curry into a large serving bowl and top with chopped coriander. (You can also put the coriander in a side dish for people to add their own. Because you know how some folks are about coriander.) And I don't think I have to be the one to tell you that steamed rice is perfect with this.

SWEET POTATO AND CARROT POTS BRÛLÉS:
Dare to Push Your Vegetables Further

___

Serves 6

2	large carrots, peeled
1	large potato, peeled
2	sweet potatoes, peeled
1/4 cup	unsalted butter, melted and cooled
3/4 cup plus	
1/4 cup	brown sugar
2	eggs, beaten
1 tbsp	chopped fresh parsley
1/4 tsp	cinnamon
1/2 tsp	baking powder
1/2 tsp	salt
	Cracked pepper

Personal vegetable puddings with a crunchy brown-sugar topping? Fancy!

1. Preheat oven to 350°F. Spray six 6-oz custard cups or ramekins with nonstick cooking spray.
2. Grate vegetables in a food processor or use your Salad Shooter (damn that Ron Popeil and his ingenious gadgets). Put the veg in a large bowl and stir in melted butter, 1/4 cup of the brown sugar, eggs, parsley, cinnamon, baking powder, salt and pepper.
3. Spoon mixture into custard cups, leaving 1/2 inch at the top. Place on a cookie sheet and bake for 35 to 40 minutes or until there's no jiggle when you wiggle.

4. Optional: Let custard cups cool off so that you can handle them. Sprinkle 2 tbsp brown sugar evenly on top of each. Get out your small blowtorch and get that sugar bubbly and browned. It will form a hard surface, ready for cracking.

TO SERVE:

Serve with a spoon and a smile.

MU SHU VEGGIES WITH
SPRING ONION MANDARIN PANCAKES:
Chinese Food for Huggers of Trees

—

Serves 4–6

Spring Onion Mandarin Pancakes:	
1 1/2 cups plus	
2 tbsp	all-purpose flour
1/4 tsp	salt
1/2 cup	boiling water
3 tbsp	cold water
3	green onions, white part only, minced
	Sesame oil
3 tbsp	vegetable oil
4	large eggs
1 tbsp plus 1 tsp	soy sauce
1 tsp	sugar
1 tsp	grated fresh ginger
1/4 tsp	pepper
1	red pepper, sliced in thin strips
2	carrots, julienned
1 cup	shredded cabbage
1	can (8 oz) sliced water chestnuts, drained
1	can (14 oz) baby corn, drained
10	button mushrooms, cut in half
2 tbsp	sake
8–10	purchased mu shu wrappers (if not making Mandarin pancakes)
1	jar hoisin sauce

This is a variation on the classic Chinese dish with the handy wrappers and cloying hoisin sauce. There are two ways to do this: the easy way, and the not so easy way. For the latter, I'm providing you with the ingredients and know-how for making homemade Mandarin pancakes as mu shu wrappers, but these can also be bought at most Asian groceries. Buying the wrappers is an excellent shortcut, although making them fresh is worth the effort. Do you have the time? The inclination? The wherewithal? Isn't it enough that you're actually cooking for your ingrate friends? Don't get me started.

1. To make the Mandarin pancakes, in a bowl, mix together 1 1/2 cups of the flour and salt. Slowly pour boiling water into flour, stirring until it starts to come together, then stir in cold water. Stir in green onion and knead in remaining 2 tbsp of the flour. Knead dough on counter until elastic, about 10 minutes, then shape into a ball, put back in bowl, cover with a damp tea towel and let sit for 20 minutes.

2. In a medium bowl, whisk together eggs, 1 tsp of the soy sauce, sugar, ginger and pepper.

3. Heat a wok or large frying pan over medium-high

heat. Add 1 tbsp of the oil, swirling wok to coat, and heat until hot but not smoking. Stir-fry egg mixture until just cooked through, about 20 seconds. Transfer eggs to a bowl and chop into bite-sized pieces.

4. Wipe the wok with some paper towel, heat it up again, add another tablespoon of oil, and swirl like before. When hot, add red pepper, carrots and cabbage; stir-fry for 1 minute. Add water chestnuts, corn and mushrooms; stir-fry for another minute. Add vegetables to bowl of cooked eggs.

5. Add remaining 1 tbsp of oil to wok and heat until hot again. Add egg and vegetable mixture, remaining 1 tbsp soy sauce and sake; stir-fry until it's all hot and yummy. Taste for seasoning. Set aside and keep warm.

6. Lightly flour work surface and, using your hands, roll dough into a rope about a foot long and an inch thick. Cut roll into 12 equal pieces. Flatten each piece with your palm, then roll into a 6-inch round. Brush one entire side of each pancake with sesame oil, then stack two pancakes together, oiled side to oiled side. You'll see why in a minute.

7. Heat a large nonstick frying pan over medium heat. Cook a couple of pancake stacks at a time, about 30 seconds on each side or until a few browning spots appear and they bubble slightly. Remove from pan and separate paired pancakes. (Drop back in the pan if not quite cooked.) You cook them in pairs because they're so delicate they would otherwise fall apart. Ancient Chinese secret. Repeat until all six stacks are cooked and you have 12 gorgeous wrappers. Keep moist and warm by covering with plastic wrap.

TO SERVE:

Put out the bowl of mu shu vegetables, lay the warm wrappers on a plate and set out a dish of hoisin sauce. Spread the luscious hoisin on a wrapper, fill with vegetable mu shu, roll and eat.

SPICY STIR-FRIED RATATOUILLE:
Veggie Lovers' Delight on a Summer's Night

—

Serves 4

2 tbsp	olive oil
2	small garlic cloves, minced
1	small Italian eggplant, peeled and cut in 1/2-inch cubes
1/2	sweet white onion, diced
2	zucchini, cut in 1/2-inch cubes
5	stalks asparagus, bottoms trimmed, cut in thirds
2	tomatoes, seeded and diced
2	portobello mushrooms, stems discarded, caps sliced
1 tbsp	fresh lemon juice
	Splash of dry vermouth
Pinch	sugar
1/2 tsp	chili flakes
	Sea salt and cracked pepper to taste
2 tbsp	chopped flat-leaf parsley
1 tbsp	chopped fresh basil

No stewy tomato mess here. Just fresh, hot, field-ripened bounty in a wok.

1. Too easy: Heat oil on high in a wok or large frying pan. Add garlic, eggplant, onion, zucchini, asparagus, tomatoes, mushrooms, lemon juice, vermouth, sugar, chili flakes, salt and pepper; stir-fry for 6 to 8 minutes or until everything is cooked and crunchy and luscious. Add parsley and basil and stir for another 30 seconds.

TO SERVE:

Dish it up and side with brown rice or slices of warm thick pita or really good earthy bread. Marrakech Almond Butter (p. 14) would be the perfect accompaniment.

CHEESE AND FRUIT AND WINE:
The Ultimate Non-Vegan Dessert

Not only is a meal-topping cheese plate the easiest no-bake dessert around, but it's also the height of sophistication. And a good cheese match can actually improve the taste of your fine wines, making you look that much better. As if that were even possible.

SOME SUGGESTIONS

Champagne and sparkling wines go best with soft cheeses such as feta and Reblochon, while Bordeaux reds and Cabernet-Merlot blends are well suited to hard cheeses such as Cheddar, Gruyère and Gouda. Riesling is mascarpone's best bud, while Sauvignon Blanc is especially good with goat cheese. Late-harvest whites sure like having the blues, as in Roquefort and Danish blue. And nothing makes a lovely port happier than a gooey Gorgonzola or Stilton. Balance your cheese board with a good selection of water crackers and crisp breads, and some sliced apples and pears, bunches of seedless grapes and plump, ripe figs. Brillat-Savarin, famed French gourmet of the early nineteenth century, wrote: "Dessert without cheese is like a pretty girl with one eye." So, here's looking at you.

I LOVE YOU

I've gone all gooey.

COCOA À GO-GO:
Tall, dark and yummy desserts

There's no greater emotional high than the sweet release of a good chocolate hit. I could go on and on about how much I love chocolate, how our codependence became a problem a while back and how we went to couples counselling and worked everything out. But I won't. Because that's private. Besides, now everything's clear skies and mellow chocolatey nights.

PERSONAL CHOCOLATE LAVA CAKES:
Because Sharing Is for Suckers

Serves 6

6 oz	bittersweet chocolate, chopped
2/3 cup	unsalted butter
3	eggs
3	egg yolks
1/4	cup sugar
1/2 tsp	vanilla
Pinch	salt
2/3 cup	all-purpose flour
2 oz	milk chocolate, chopped in chunks
	Crème fraîche (see sidebar) (optional)
	Icing sugar (optional)
	Fresh berries (optional)

Warning: this is an à la minute dessert, so if you lack the confidence level of preparing molten cakes for your guests as they're tucking into your other delectable comestibles, this ain't the recipe for you, sister. But the batter can be made a bit in advance. And they're sooo worth the stress. Besides, you should really learn to relax a bit. We've been talking and we all think you take yourself too seriously.

1. Preheat oven to 325°F. Butter and flour six 6-oz ramekins or custard cups.
2. Melt bittersweet chocolate with butter (slowly in microwave or gently on the stove over low heat). Stir until smooth. Set aside to cool slightly.
3. Get out a big bowl. Using a hand mixer, or your inherent physical prowess, beat whole eggs and egg yolks with sugar until pale yellow and thick. This will take a solid 8 to 10 minutes. Stir in vanilla and salt. Little by little add the flour. Finally, add the chocolate-butter mixture and beat another few minutes, until smooth and glossy.
4. Divide half the batter among the ramekins. Divide milk chocolate chunks among the ramekins, putting them in the centre of the batter and poking them in a bit with your finger. Top each ramekin with remaining choco batter.

5. Place ramekins on a cookie sheet and bake for 15 to 18 minutes or until the tops poof up a bit and the centres wiggle like your ass in a thong (note: just the right amount).

6. Let cool for 2 minutes, then run a sharp knife around the edges of each ramekin. Flip them out onto six waiting dessert plates.

TO SERVE:

They don't need a damn thing, but if you want to gild the lily, sprinkle with some icing sugar, or side with a dollop of crème fraîche or some fresh berries.

HOW TO MAKE CRÈME FRAÎCHE

Mix 1 cup whipping cream with 1/4 cup buttermilk. Stir to combine, cover and let stand at room temperature for the better part of the day, then put in the fridge for 24 hours. Can be left as is or whipped a bit to make thicker.

THE PURPLE PROWLER AND THE PRINCE'S TOE:
A Bedtime Story (Serve with Chocolate Chunk Cookies)

by AMY ROSEN

Many moons ago, on a Saturday night, a young Prince's parents went to a very chic nightclub in the town square to get lightheaded. When they returned home early the next morning, they found their child quite horrified and anguished with pain. This young lad was clutching his foot. Tender as they could— "This little piggy went to market, this little piggy stayed home"—they pulled away each of his tiny blood-stained fingers.

With the disengaging of the child's hand from his foot, it became apparent that he was missing his big toe. "Yikes!" yelped the stately Queen.

"What foul and evil thing has done this to my princely child?" bellowed the King.

What the royal couple did not know was that miles away, in the Tanglewood forests off the Fen-Slopes, lived the Purple Prowler. This gnome-like creature was actually quite a nice shade of purple. Two horns protruded harshly from his furrowed brow, and quite sharp were these horns. It was a quick shake of the head that had done the dastardly deed to the poor Prince's foot.

Why did the Prince not react to the dismembering of his toe? How could he be beaten by this wretched foe? The answer to this question I'm afraid I do not know. But believe me, he later regretted not giving the crusty-nosed varmint a good slap on the cheek.

No time before or since did the hills screech with laughter as they did that foul evening the young Prince's toe was won. A little ritual the Purple Prowler did perform—a cute tap number (which included the use of flaming sparklers and a neon Hula Hoop), followed by a blues ditty on the saxophone.

Oh so proud of his night's ravages was this fire-eyed beast that he went knocking on the neighbouring monsters' hollows at all hours of that eve and, in fine fettle, dangled the Prince's toe in front of their envious eyes.

After gallivanting around for the greater part of that fateful Saturday night, the Purple Prowler retired to his home, placing the discoloured toe in a golden box, where it would remain for some twenty years to come.

Twenty years later, on the day of his twenty-third birthday, the Prince decided to propose marriage to the fair maiden whom he had been courting for some five years. He dashed over to his love's castle and popped the question.

"Of course, my love" was her answer to the Prince. "Nothing would make me happier than to live and work beside you forevermore." The Prince, however, didn't seem wholly satisfied with this answer. Something was amiss.

"Actually, my sweet," he replied, "I have reconsidered my proposal, for I walk with a hobble. I shall retrieve the toe that I lost as a child, and only then shall I be yours forevermore."

"The toe, you say," queried the maiden. "You say you will wed me only when thoust reattaches thine toe? But, my prince, I love thee as thou art. Long ago a foe stole your toe. Now I beseech thee—let it go!"

"My sweet," said the Prince, "this is the one last deed I shall do to prove my love for thee. A perfect Prince thou shall wed, but ne'er with a lame one shall thee share a bed."

So off to the Fen-Slopes dashed the handsome Prince, to retrieve his toe, lost so long ago . . .

A fortnight later he arrived at the door of the devilish gnome. "Excuse me, little purple man," said the dashing Prince. "That toe of mine you possess, I want it back."

"I knew some day this time would come," grinned the Purple Prowler. "And I have prepared well for your arrival. Tea biscuit?"

"Swords, daggers, bow and arrow, by what means do you choose to meet your death, you wine-coloured dwarf?"

"A war of the wits," snivelled the horned man.

"Hmm, interesting concept," observed the Prince. "I'm up for it."

"Splendid. Riddle number one: I have four wheels, plastic to the core, you jump upon my board and we roll across the floor. What am I?"

"That is easy! I know you to be the Purple Prowler," answered the Prince. "Now I have a question for thee. What is bigger than a breadbox but smaller than a house?"

"You!" replied the dark dweller. "As well as myself, and these chairs, and the throw rug, and the portrait of Mother, the cauldron . . ."

And so it was that this battle of the wits, or nitwits, lasted and lasted, on through the night and into the years. The feud was neverending, and the poor Prince never wed. The fair maiden, on the other hand, married a one-armed man from a neighbouring village and lived happily ever after.

It is said that if one walks the Tanglewood forests off of the Fen-Slopes, late at night, questions of trivia may still be heard in the air . . .

"What is dead or alive, here or there, and can be found everywhere?"

"Why, the earth! And candles, and birds, books, kittens, bees, popsicles . . ."

A-HEY NONNY NONNY AND HEAVEN FORFEND, THERE BE NASTY BUSINESS AFOOT

CHOCOLATE CHUNK COOKIES:
The '80s Fave Makes a Crunchy Comeback

—

Makes about 40 cookies

1/2 cup	vegetable shortening
1/2 cup	unsalted butter, softened
1 cup	brown sugar
1/2 cup	white sugar
2	eggs, beaten
1 tsp	vanilla
1 1/4	cups all-purpose flour
1 tsp	salt
1/2 tsp	baking soda
8	squares (each 1 oz) semi-sweet baking chocolate

SNACKING TIP

Why bother with baking the cookies? After all, raw cookie dough is the queen of snack-stuffs. Simply load dough into a freezer container, then defrost and eat as needed.

One bowl, one spoon, a pan and an oven. No Mixmaster required, because if you're like me, you don't have one. Just good upper body strength and the will to make delicious cookies.

1. Preheat oven to 375°F. Spray a cookie sheet with nonstick cooking spray.

2. In a large bowl, mix together shortening and butter. Add brown and white sugar. Beat with a wooden spoon for a solid 2 minutes until there are no lumps and the batter is smooth, not grainy. Add eggs and vanilla; stir to combine. Add in flour, salt and baking soda. Stir away. You now have cookie batter.

3. Cut each square of chocolate into about six pieces. Throw the chunks into the batter, being careful not to let too many accidentally fall into your mouth. Stir to combine.

4. Using your hands, roll dough into 1-inch balls, and place on cookie sheet 4 by 4, at equal distances apart. Bake for 10 to 12 minutes or until golden brown. Let rest for a minute, then remove from tray and let cool on a wire rack.

TO SERVE:

I usually like to stuff three in my mouth at a time. A highball of icy milk is a must.

TOBLERONE CHUNK BROWNIES:
The Perfect Substitute for Affection

Boyfriend stopped calling? Cat ran away? Vibrator on the fritz? Don't fret, brownies are always there for you, like a warm, chocolatey hug. (And next time keep extra batteries on hand.)

5 oz	semisweet chocolate
1/2 cup	unsalted butter
3	eggs
1 cup	sugar
1/4 cup	cocoa powder
1 tsp	vanilla
Pinch	salt
1 1/4 cups	all-purpose flour
1	Toblerone bar (100 g), each triangle chopped in about three chunks
1/2 cup	hazelnuts, toasted and roughly chopped (optional)

1. Preheat oven to 350°F. Spray an 8-inch square cake pan with nonstick cooking spray.
2. Over low heat on the stove or in the microwave, melt together semisweet chocolate and butter. They'll seem like oil and water at first, but stir gently and they will come together and look nice and shiny. Set aside to cool.
3. In a large bowl, beat eggs until good and frothy. Stir in sugar, cocoa powder, vanilla and salt. Stir in melted chocolate and butter. Stir in flour, making sure there are no lumps, then stir in Toblerone chunks and hazelnuts, if using.
4. Pour batter into cake pan and bake for 30 to 35 minutes. Poke a knife in the middle (avoiding chocolate chunks). If it comes out clean, they're ready to come out.

BAKING TIP:
To chop nuts without having them roll all over the floor, load them into a resealable plastic bag, zip it up and pound with a heavy implement, such as a pan. Better to take your frustrations out on these nuts than your boyfriend's.

TO SERVE:
Pull up a chair to the counter and dig in. Or cut into 16 squares and share.

DOUBLE-DIPPED STRAWBERRIES:
What's Black and White and Red All Over?

—

Makes 1 pint

1 pint	unhulled strawberries, at room temperature
5 oz	good-quality semisweet chocolate, chopped
3 oz	white chocolate, chopped

I thought I was so clever. I was having friends over to test my recipes, and as I was dipping some big luscious berries into melted chocolate, I thought, Hey, what about dunking them in white chocolate after? Cool. So I make these gorgeous mouthfuls, giddy at the prospect of presenting the crazy black-and-white berries to my duly impressed friends. After all, it's not every day someone creates a new taste sensation. So I bring them out and everyone chimes in, "Oh, tuxedo strawberries!" Turns out everyone but me had eaten these before. And during subsequent trips following my culinary "discovery" I ate them off dessert buffets from North Carolina to Jamaica. Still, in my mind, these are my babies. But I also take credit for inventing sunless tanning, so there you go.

1. Line a cookie sheet with foil. Pat strawberries dry if need be. If they're wet when you dip them, the chocolate will slide off when it cools down.
2. Melt the semisweet chocolate slowly (either in the microwave or over low heat on the stove). Stir until smooth.
3. Grab a berry by the stem and dip in chocolate three-quarters up the berry. Place dipped berries on cookie sheet and put in fridge to cool. When chocolate is hard (about 20 minutes), slowly melt white chocolate, take berries out of

fridge and dip in melted white chocolate so that the white covers about half of the dark chocolate. Back in the fridge they go until you're ready to eat them.

TO SERVE:

A bite for you, a bite for your partner . . . then you might want to get out the dipped berries. Heh heh.

CLASSIC CHOCOLATE MOUSSE:
The Spoonable Chocolate Fix

Serves 6

5 oz	semisweet chocolate (the better your chocolate, the better your mousse)
1/4 cup	water
1/2 tsp	vanilla
4	eggs, separated
1/2 cup	sugar
Pinch	salt
1	canister whipped cream

This is one of the first desserts I ever learned how to make, way back in the early 1980s, when pregnant women, the elderly and wee tots were still blissfully chowing down on foods containing raw eggs, raw meat and unpasteurized cheeses (now, newly cool). Here's to an old stalwart that has remained delicious through the ages. But sorry, little Timmy, now we know better, so this chocolate yum-yum is for Mommy.

1. Slowly melt chocolate with water in the microwave or on the stove over low heat. Stir in vanilla and set aside to cool.

2. In a large bowl, beat egg yolks (electric mixer is best), gradually adding sugar. Mixture should be pale yellow and thick and fall in ribbons when you're there. Mix in cooled chocolate until blended.

3. In another very clean bowl, beat egg whites with salt until stiff peaks form. (If the whisk or beater or bowl is dirty or any sugar or fat has contaminated your utensils or the eggs, they won't whip up and you'll have to start again. I'm sorry. This is life in the big city.)

4. Stir a dollop of stiff egg whites into chocolate mixture to get things moving, then gently but thoroughly fold in the remaining whites until it all looks good and chocolatey. Cover and chill for a few hours or, better still, overnight.

TO SERVE:

There are two ways you could go here: spoon it into parfait cups or martini glasses or ramekins, then top them with a retro spritz of whipped cream, or serve it in a big bowl topped by a mound of whipped cream. It's all a matter of personal style and taste. Do what feels right.

FOOD STYLE

We all know there's fashionable food (this book is chock full of it!) – but what about food AS fashion?

Poached jumbo shrimp – smart dangly earrings
Leftover prosciutto – makeshift meat bra
Strawberry coulis – edible crotchless panties
Cherry Kool-Aid – quick hair colour boost
Baked brie wheel – kicky French chapeau

WHITE CHOCOLATE BERRY TART:
It's Not Really Chocolate, but I Still Call It Friend

Serves 10–12

25	social tea biscuits (approx)
3/4 cup	unsalted butter, 1/2 cup melted and 1/4 cup at room temperature
1 lb	white chocolate, chopped
2/3 cup	whipping cream
1/2 tsp	vanilla
1 pint	fresh raspberries
	Extra raspberries and whipped cream, for garnish (optional)

I'm not a huge fan of white chocolate, but this tart, inspired by a dessert from one of my favourite Italian restaurants in Toronto, changed my mind about the chocolate imposter. It doesn't have the same effect on me as its dark kissing cousins, but it certainly satisfies a summertime sweet tooth.

1. Preheat oven to 400°F. Grease a 10-inch ceramic tart pan or springform pan.

2. Pound tea biscuits into small crumbs by putting them in a plastic bag and crushing with a rolling pin or wine bottle, or pulse in a food processor. You should have 2 cups of crumbs. Stir in the melted butter and firmly pat into tart pan. Bake until lightly browned, 10 to 15 minutes. Let cool in pan.

3. In a saucepan over low heat or in the microwave, slowly melt white chocolate and remaining 1/4 cup butter together; stir in cream and vanilla, stirring until smooth and glossy—no lumps! Set aside to cool slightly.

4. Layer cooled tart crust with fresh raspberries, then pour white chocolate mixture over top. Refrigerate for at least 3 hours, but better overnight.

TO SERVE:

A perfect little slice is gorgeous on its own, but I wouldn't say no to a few extra fresh berries and a little whipped cream on the side. Slice with a wet knife for perfect wedges.

DON'T LIKE SURPRISES? READ THE RECIPE AHEAD OF TIME.

Needs to chill for 3 hours, bake for 2 or rest overnight. Who knew? You would have if you planned ahead. Reading the recipe ahead of time could make the difference between a successful gourmet dinner party that shall be remembered and referred to through the ages . . . and ordering an emergency pizza on the fly.

FLOURLESS CHOCOLATE TORTE:
Easy as Pie

—

Serves 8–10

1 lb	bittersweet chocolate (the good stuff, like Valrhona, or even premium supermarket name brands, like President's Choice or Master's Choice. The better the chocolate, the better the cake. That's all I'm saying.)
1 1/2 cups	unsalted butter, at room temperature
1 cup	sugar
1 cup	ground almonds (this equals a 100 g pkg)
2 tbsp	Amaretto (optional)
2 tsp	vanilla
6	large eggs, separated
Pinch	salt
	Icing sugar or whipped cream, for garnish (optional)

A day without chocolate is like a day without sunshine. And a day without sunshine isn't really much of a day.

1. Preheat oven to 300°F. Spray a 9-inch springform cake pan with nonstick cooking spray.

2. Break up or chop chocolate, place in a bowl and microwave on Medium for short intervals until melted, stirring in between and being careful that it doesn't burn. Burning happens easier than you'd think. If you don't have a microwave, melt chocolate in a pan over low heat, stirring often. When melted, take off heat and stir in butter, sugar, almonds, Amaretto and vanilla.

3. Beat egg yolks until they are a bit thicker and bright yellow. Stir into cooling chocolate mixture.

4. Beat egg whites with salt until they form stiff peaks, then fold them into the chocolate mixture a little at a time until you've got a nice even chocolatey batter.

5. Home stretch: Pour batter into springform pan and bake for about 1 hour. The middle will rise and crack a bit, but that's fine. Let cool in pan to room temperature.

TO SERVE:

Remove sides from pan. The torte will be quite moist, so slicing with a wet knife is advisable. Sprinkle the whole thing with icing sugar or top each slice with a dollop of whipped cream. Serving each slice with a shot glass of milk is both trendy and useful. This baby's gonna make you sweat.

MEMORY LANE

Madeline and Emily, my two little nieces, have an Easy-Bake Oven. But it is the same Easy-Bake as the avocado-green number from my youth in name only. Now called the Easy-Bake Oven and Snack Center, it looks like a little white microwave, complete with faux-digital cooking panel. The 100-watt bulb remains a necessity and those two little round metal cake tins are still shoved in the side slot, but now there's a snappy pink pan pusher. In addition to the wholesome baked goodies we've come to love over the years, now you can also make nachos, chocolate-dipped pretzels and caramel corn. Now that's progress.

INDEX